Jury Nullified

How judges are able to influence the outcome of a criminal trial

David T. Kaye, Esq.

Copyright 2019

Author: David T. Kaye, Esq.

Publisher: David Taylor Kaye

ISBN 978-0-578-42820-8

Lulu printing

Biography:

David Kaye is a graduate of the University of California, San Diego, with a Bachelors of Arts degree in Economics. He obtained his law degree from Western State University in December of 1993, and was admitted to the California State Bar in 1994. He subsequently sought admission and was accepted into the United States District Court, Southern District. Mr. Kaye worked as a Law Clerk for a Superior Court Judge in Orange County, and worked as a Law Clerk for the Office of the United States Attorney in San Diego. He then served as a Deputy District Attorney in Tulare County located in Central California. Mr. Kaye left the public sector and established a private practice limited to Family Law and Criminal Law, with an emphasis on trial work. For thirteen years Mr. Kaye was Of Counsel with the Law Offices of Myles L. Berman and represented clients at trial. Mr. Kaye also was trial counsel for the Law Offices of Eugene Ellis for nearly a decade. Mr. Kaye has been active in the legal community and served four years as Co-Chairman of the Criminal Section of the San Diego North County Bar Association. Mr. Kaye has represented more than 4,000 criminal clients and has personally tried more than 250 jury trials throughout every County in Southern California. He was routinely retained by other law firms to represent their clients at trial.

A special thanks to Scott, Taylor, Chris, and Andrea for their help and support.

Jury Nullified

How judges are able to influence the outcome of a criminal trial

David T. Kaye, Esq.

Forward:

Forward

Many books have been written over the years about jury trials. Some of the most well known trial attorneys in the country have authored books about famous high profile cases. There are humorous lawyer joke books, and books about various captivating and sensational trials. There are authoritative books by authors with unquestionably impressive pedigree and credentials, and there are scholarly legal treatises where each page contains more citations than text.

Jury Nullified is none of these. Jury Nullified is a book written by a veteran trial attorney who spent more than two decades wearing out the leather of his shoes traveling from courthouse to courthouse engaged in trial. In this book the author shares a unique perspective and the opportunity to compare and contrast the manner in which different judges preside over criminal jury trials, and the impact those differences can make on the outcome of the trial.

Chapter 1: A Little Background on the Sixth Amendment

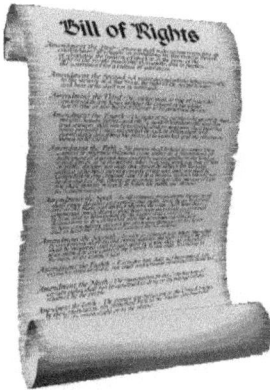

No idea is more central to our judicial system than the concept of trial by jury. Citizens of the United States need not be fearful of a trial outcome determined by the King, or Star Chamber, or blue ribbon panel, or land owners, or some other elite sanctioned body. Citizens will decide the legal fate of citizens.

The United States Constitution has represented the foundation of the United States of America since March 04, 1789. The Constitution has only been Amended twenty-seven times since its inception almost two hundred and thirty years ago. The first ten amendments are collectively referred to as the Bill of Rights. Proposed to assuage the fears of Anti-Federalists who had opposed Constitutional ratification, these Amendments guarantee a number of personal freedoms, limit the government's power in judicial and other proceedings, and reserve some powers to the states and the public. Originally the Amendments applied only to the Federal Government, however, most were subsequently applied to the government of each state by way of the Fourteenth Amendment, through a process known as incorporation.

The Sixth Amendment to the United States Constitution holds that:

> In all criminal prosecutions, the accused shall enjoy the right to a speedy and public trial, by an impartial jury. . . .

Today the concept of a trial by jury in the United States is commonly understood and is ingrained in our culture. The concept of the jury trial is represented everywhere in our society and is depicted in movies, television, and even pop songs have lyrics about the jury. Social media is now playing a role in depicting sensational jury trials and high profile cases. Although jury trials are quite common in civil trials, they are particularly important in criminal trials because in criminal trials a person can be deprived of their liberty or life - Jail or Execution!

Citizens are called upon by the government to act as jurors in criminal matters. They appear at the courthouse for jury duty after receiving some sort of jury summons. Jurors appear at the courthouse and are identified, assembled, processed by a jury commissioner, or other courthouse official, and sent off to an awaiting courtroom for service.

Jurors bring a lifetime of experiences with them to the courtroom. Most have an opinion about various high profile cases such as the O. J. Simpson trial. Many have heard about some of the Innocence Project successes where citizens, who were previously convicted by a jury, are subsequently released from death row, or decades of incarceration, after evidence establishes their factual innocence. They have seen videos of law enforcement misconduct, and usually have been the victims of some sort of crime. All of these life experiences are brought to the courtroom by jurors who will be asked to decide the case.

There are many specific jury instructions, but essentially jurors are told by the judge in the courtroom to accept the relevant law as given to them by the judge, sort through the facts as determined by them throughout the trial by the evidence presented, and apply some sort of common sense analysis to reach a verdict. In a criminal trial the verdict must be unanimous and each juror must affirm their verdict. Jurors are told by the judge that in order to convict and reach a verdict of guilty, they must be convinced of guilt beyond a reasonable doubt.

Jury nullification is not a new concept, but it is a term that really came into vogue after the infamous O. J. Simpson trial, although the term has been modified somewhat from its true meaning. Jury nullification involves a jury acquitting a criminal defendant who is technically guilty, but who does not deserve punishment in the minds of the jurors. It seems that most people use the term to describe a situation where they believe the defendant is guilty, but the jury mistakenly reaches a verdict of not guilty. The idea that the verdict of not guilty is being reached because the jurors do not believe the defendant should be held criminally liable seems to have been lost. The vast majority of people believe that O. J. Simpson was guilty, and that he deserved punishment for the murders, and that the jury reached the wrong verdict.

Jury nullification might occur in a marijuana use case or a prostitution case. The prosecutor proves the marijuana use, or the prostitution. The judge instructs on the law making it

3

illegal to use marijuana or to engage in sexual acts for money. But the jurors return a verdict of not guilty because they do not personally believe marijuana use or prostitution should be illegal, and that the government should not be involved in criminal prosecutions for those crimes, due to the belief that these are victimless crimes. In fact, these two crimes present such difficulty for prosecutors that prospective jurors are often asked about their feelings regarding these crimes, prior to being selected as jurors to hear these types of cases.

To nullify something is to make it legally null and void, or to invalidate something. Nullifying a jury would be to cause the jury to lose its value, or to render the jury ineffective. I use the term "jury nullified," to suggest that the role of the jury can be made null and void by the presiding trial judge if certain efforts are made to steer the jury toward a desired outcome.

Many judicial officers view the jury with contempt. They feel they are much smarter than the collective jurors. They know they have more experience. They believe they are less likely to become confused by complicated evidence. They are convinced they are less likely to become fooled by prosecution or defense trial tactics. They are confident in their own mind that they could reach a "correct" verdict faster and more reliably than the jury.

This brand of judicial arrogance reminds us of the original concerns which created the need for the Bill of Rights protections provided for in the United States Constitution.

Chapter 2: Meet the Players

You can't understand the game unless you understand the players. Each player in a jury trial comes into the process with different backgrounds and vastly different agendas. The prosecutor and defense attorney are participants in an adversarial process with polar opposite agendas, although they would both probably claim to be seeking justice. In a criminal case, loss of liberty (jail) and loss of life (execution) can be at stake, so a trial is a serious matter with serious consequences.

The Prosecutor: Champion of the People

The prosecutor is an attorney working for the government and is there at trial seeking to obtain a conviction. In a criminal case the prosecutor works closely with the arresting law enforcement agency to present all of the incriminating evidence which establishes guilt of the crime. Prosecutors come in many shapes and sizes but there is some obvious commonality among them.

First, to be a successful prosecutor you must publicly affirm that being a prosecutor is not just a job but is a lifelong calling. If you espouse less than zeal for being a lifelong prosecutor you are unlikely to be hired by the prosecution agencies. If you express less than zeal once hired, you might quickly find yourself assigned to a less than desirable position such as juvenile prosecutions. There are many stories of top Harvard Law School graduates who decide they want to spend some time contributing to the community by working in the prosecutor's office, only to find themselves rejected. The top brass in the office who do the hiring are the true believers, and they do not want to spend

5

time and money training part-timers and heretics who might publicly renounce the word of law enforcement and righteousness. There are two sides to every story in their mind. There is the officer's story, and then there is the defendant's story, which they know is a total lie.

If you accept the proposition that some law enforcement officers might lie, exaggerate, or manufacture evidence, then you are probably not a strong viable candidate for the prosecutor's office. If you believe that all law enforcement officers are well trained, highly skilled, brave men and women who have sworn to protect and serve our community to the best of their abilities, then drink a little more of the purple Kool-Aid and welcome aboard. Obviously, I'm being overly simplistic and numerous and varied beliefs are held by prosecutors, but generally defense attorneys and prosecutors are at the polar extremes of the spectrum. Think of the relationship between prosecutors and defense attorneys as similar to that of conservatives and liberals, or Democrats and Republicans, or even cats and dogs at times.

I was first a prosecutor and then a defense attorney, which sort of makes me like Switzerland in some sense. Some defense attorneys have concerns about me because they know I am a former prosecutor, and some prosecutors have concerns because many believe in their heart that I "betrayed them" and switched to the "dark side" to use their verbiage.

Moving from prosecutor to defense attorney is generally much easier than moving from defense attorney to prosecutor because it is very difficult to be hired by any prosecution office if you are a criminal defense attorney. Again, the top brass almost universally do not like defense attorneys despite the smokescreen of courthouse professionalism.

One of the common prosecution office job interview trick questions involves asking the job applicant why they want to be a prosecutor. The applicant will enthusiastically respond by explaining that they enjoy criminal law, and the excitement of jury trials, and maybe even something about helping the community. The next question is then about their willingness to work in the Office of the Public Defender as a defense attorney if all of that is true. Anyone who does not see the trap and indicates that they are open to working as a defense attorney fails the test and is considered by almost all of the top brass to be a less desirable applicant.

The Defense Attorney

Criminal defense attorneys represent the citizens charged with violating the law. The defense attorney may choose to present exculpatory evidence at trial which establishes innocence, or the defense attorney may choose to merely scrutinize the prosecution evidence attempting to establish that the evidence presented is inadequate under the law to establish guilt, according to the legal standard, which is guilt beyond a reasonable doubt.

Some might ask, "What kind of scum bag would defend a guilty person who committed a crime?" The issue for trial of course is whether the defendant is guilty of committing a crime. Our system of justice requires far more for guilt than being arrested by law enforcement and being charged with a crime by the local prosecutor.

The word scum means a low, worthless, or an evil person. Despite their phony courtroom professionalism which includes smiles, handshakes, and courtesy, this is what many prosecutors truly feel about criminal defense attorneys. A few prosecutors are openly hostile toward defense attorneys but they are careful to maintain civility and avoid crossing any boundaries. I remember meeting a veteran prosecutor for a trial that I had never met before. The prosecutor refused to shake my hand when I introduced myself. I was so freaked out (a common legal term) by the incident that I researched this prosecutor and learned that there were several Court of Appeals cases involving him relating to prosecutorial misconduct. One case involved the prosecutor trying to kick all the minorities off the jury. He was a true believer in every sense of the word.

Similarly, many defense attorneys despise prosecutors to a certain extent. They are always ready to share a story of a reasonable prosecutor and a reasonable case outcome, but then they also have their complaint list. The word "Nazi" for some reason seems to be a common word of choice. I never quite understood the analogy between being a member of the National Socialist German Worker's party and being a criminal prosecutor, but I know it's no compliment and I've heard the word countless times. Maybe the meaning is that the prosecutor (a Nazi party member) is blindly following the orders of a madman like Hitler (top brass in the prosecutor's office) to prosecute the case no matter how objectively outrageous. Anyway, it just doesn't sound very flattering to me, and when I hear the term I take care to avoid disclosing that I used to be a prosecutor.

The dichotomy between prosecutors and defense attorneys can be much worse than Democrats and Republicans in a heated election year, although there are loving spouses who vote for competing party candidates. A juror is generally not aware of the relationship between the parties unless they start bickering and feuding in front of the jury.

Although many Democrats and Republicans are able to cooperate and get along despite their divergent starting points and differing philosophies, there can always be that underlying distrust. It is difficult to make sweeping generalizations, but criminal defense attorneys and prosecutors are almost always very different types of people with differing beliefs, and very different roles in the courtroom.

Most people do not fully appreciate the role of the criminal defense attorney. Being a criminal defense attorney is not about "beating the charges" and helping guilty people "get off." Being a criminal defense attorney is mostly about providing legal assistance and sage advice to clients who are charged with various crimes, safeguarding the integrity of the criminal judicial process, and acting as a deterrent to prosecutorial abuses.

Imagine that a citizen retains a defense attorney after being arrested for possession of drugs - for the third time. The role of the defense attorney is not to immediately assert that the drugs were planted by crooked cops out to frame an innocent man. The defense attorney will typically follow a systematic process for establishing the facts and resolving the matter. As a formality, the defense attorney would appear in court with his client and would enter a plea of not guilty to the charges. People seem confused by this, but it makes no sense to plead guilty at this point until it can be ascertained if the prosecution has sufficient evidence to establish guilt.

The defense attorney would normally make some type of information request from the prosecution in order to obtain the chemical test results, and a copy of the police report. After reviewing the lab results and police reports, the defense attorney would meet with his client to discuss the matter. Some clients might candidly admit to possessing the drugs, and others will swear that the drugs belonged to someone else, or were planted, which could be a remote possibility. The defense attorney might then explain to his client that the information in the police report appears to establish guilt because the chemical lab results confirm the sample was crack cocaine, and the police report indicates that the client admitted to the police that the crack belonged to him. The client immediately responds that he only told the police it was his crack is because the police promised him more crack if he admitted that the crack belonged to him. Yes, this is what he said. The defense attorney now knows that the case is not defensible at trial, and that his client is unlikely to be a credible witness at trial, and that the attorney needs a more paternalistic approach to help the client achieve the best outcome. The defense attorney demands that his client immediately enroll in a residential drug treatment program.

Next, the defense attorney contacts the prosecutor and discusses a resolution. But the prosecutor is tired of this third time drug user and wants three years in prison and so no agreements are reached.

At the first settlement conference the prosecutor and the defense attorney make their best sales presentations to the settlement judge. Each side explains their positions and their opinion about a reasonable outcome for the case. The defense attorney is well prepared and has a "good guy" package ready to give to the judge, which includes all of the client's volunteer work, charity work, employment history, family history, and explains that the client "wants treatment and voluntarily chose to enroll in a residential drug treatment facility." Although there was some prodding, and the primary motivation was to avoid jail, the client did agree to treatment and does want treatment.

The prosecutor refuses to negotiate or reduce the charges to a lesser offense because this is the third drug offense. Having the more serious offense on the client's record really doesn't damage his employment opportunities since he already has a criminal record with two felony charges for possession of drugs. But, the prosecutor is impressed with the drug program and agrees to let the client stay in the program since he really wants the defendant to work on his drug problem to avoid future problems and cases.

The judge agrees to allow the client to remain in the four month drug program, and then serve six months in jail upon successful completion of the drug program.

This is an example of the role of the criminal defense attorney. The defense attorney didn't "beat the charges," and didn't "get his client off." However, after evaluating the case and the evidence, the defense attorney dissuaded his client from pursuing an ill-advised path of denying his confession and blaming the drugs on others. The defense attorney persuaded his client to seek immediate treatment, presented his client in the most favorable and sympathetic manner possible to the judge and the prosecutor, and achieved the best possible outcome for client.

The client spent four months in treatment and then six

months in jail. If the client had not hired an attorney to assist him, he would have surely spent at least three years in prison after the judge heard his ridiculous story and sentenced him accordingly for his lack of remorse, honesty, and acceptance of responsibility.

The Friendly, Honest Bailiff

The courtroom bailiff is a law enforcement officer assigned to maintain the security of the courtroom and is conspicuously visible in the courtroom throughout the trial. A few courthouses are trying to cut costs by using community officers, but generally sworn law enforcement work as bailiffs.

In a criminal trial the parties are instructed not to have any contact with the jurors because of the possibility of influence and to avoid any perception of influence. Therefore, it is the bailiff who principally interacts with the jurors during the course of the trial when not in session.

The bailiff is usually assigned to the same courtroom with the same judge and they develop some type professional working relationship. The bailiff might not be a close friend and might not be invited to dinner, but at some point the bailiff learns the expectations and general philosophy of the judge. The bailiff will know whether the judge is a former prosecutor, or whether the judge makes disparaging remarks about various criminal defense attorneys, and his conduct will undoubtedly reflect those observations to an extent.

In a criminal trial some type of law enforcement officer will usually be called as a witness by the prosecutor. A portion of the defense might involve an attack of that officer as untruthful, mistaken, aggressive, or incompetent. Therefore, one of the considerations for a judge is to ensure that his bailiff exhibits behavior which is the antithesis of these attacks. The bailiff should be friendly, professional, courteous, intelligent, and well spoken. It just doesn't matter to most lay jurors that the witness works for the police and the bailiff is a sheriff, or that the bailiff is a different human being than the arresting officer. Jurors with little close interaction with law enforcement officers will almost universally associate some sort of feeling about the courtroom bailiff with some sort of opinion about the arresting officer. It's the strangest phenomenon but an experienced trial judge is aware of it and picking the wrong bailiff could help the defense.

So if the criminal case involves a battery upon a peace officer during the arrest, the courtroom bailiff will know, explicitly or implicitly, that the judge wants him to go out of his way to be cordial, courteous, and friendly to the jurors.

If the criminal case involves charges of violence, the bailiff might hover over the defendant and seem concerned by every furtive gesture and movement and noise. By watching the bailiff one might easily conclude that the defendant posed a serious threat to the courtroom security and was a dangerous and violent person. Oh wait, the charges the jury will be asked to decide involve violence by the defendant. Notice that the bailiff never said a word to the jurors and the record does not reveal any indication of bias or influence, and yet the judge's courtroom bailiff has communicated something about the defendant to the jurors.

As the jurors sit patiently in the courthouse hallway waiting to start their day the bailiff might make a point to tell the jurors with a sigh and a look of disappointment, "We are just waiting for the defense again." A subtle message has been sent about the defense attorney but certainly not enough to concern the appellate court about an unfair trial. The judge's bailiff is making an intentional, conscious decision to tell the jurors that it is the defense who is making them wait instead of telling them that we will be starting shortly, or telling them that we have been delayed and expect to start in a few minutes, or telling them generically that we are waiting on the attorneys to start. A very subtle advantage has been gained on the long road toward steering the jury.

The prosecutor's office is usually in the same government building as the courthouse, or it might be conveniently located across the street. The defense attorney might be located somewhere in the neighborhood, or might be across town, or might even be out of the county, which creates a situation where the defense attorney seems to run late more than the prosecution.

Can I borrow a piece of chalk? Counsel, it's not my job to provide you with supplies the bailiff tells the defense attorney. But there is a large six-foot high chalk board in the courtroom which I expected to use to present my case to the jury. Surely you have some broken pieces of chalk in your desk drawer or there are supplies in the back hallway. Sorry counsel! The bailiff barks like a military drill sergeant as he squares up to the defense attorney and his hand slides down his right thigh nearer to his gun. You should have brought chalk! The prosecutors use the county courthouse chalkboard regularly and the bailiff knows exactly where the chalk is kept because he keeps it in his desk drawer. The courtroom bailiff is almost always assigned to a particular courtroom with the same judge and they have a close working relationship and the bailiff is well aware of the judge's philosophy and mindset. The defense attorney quickly scrambles to revise his presentation which is now not quite as polished as it would have been had he used the chalkboard as anticipated. Another cumulative incremental advantage for the prosecution has been achieved when both parties are trying to persuade the jury.

How about another bailiff story? . I had trial once where I tried to engage the bailiff in some water-cooler type, friendly chatter. There was almost no response and the bailiff was clearly trying to ignore me. The situation quickly became awkward. Since I was going to spend about a week in the courtroom with this guy I asked him if everything was okay just to clear the air. The bailiff stopped what he was doing, which was reading the paper, and peered at me through his reading glasses telling me that, "Everything is fine. I just don't like defense attorneys." Holy Shit! This is gonna be a long week. I could hardly wait to meet the judge that allowed or encouraged this "Adam Henry" (cop slang for Ass Hole).

I did what any self-respecting man of principle would do under the circumstance. I immediately broke into a story about being a former prosecutor and agreed with him about defense attorneys. When in Rome, do as the Romans do.

I should mention that I have met many friendly and professional bailiffs who are very pleasant and offer me every courtesy. They ask if I want water. They ask if I need anything. They mention the bathroom in the back hallway for the attorneys to use. It's like flying first class. The week was filled with nothing but mutual respect, daily pleasantries, and a few funny jokes when we are in a recess

15

and out of the presence of the jury. And guess what type of judge is on the bench? With this type of a bailiff, the judge is almost always a fair and impartial straight shooter who just calls balls and strikes and gives everyone an honest trial and lets the jury decide.

The court reporter:

The court reporter is the stenographer who usually sits near the front of the judges' bench at that funny little machine typing some sort of morse code that only they can understand. If requested to do so at a later time, they can produce a certified transcript of everything that was said during a proceeding or trial. Some courthouses use audio recordings of the courtroom proceedings and trials with a monitor supervising the recording process, and later the recordings can be transcribed if necessary.

Now generally the court reporter is just a neutral recorder of the facts and has almost no opportunity to editorialize or influence the jury. But you can image the significance between a transcript that reads, "I killed the man" as opposed to "I did NOT kill the man". Potentially all those present in the courtroom would submit sworn declarations attesting to the fact that the witness clearly testified that he did NOT kill the man and that the court reporter's transcript is erroneous.

How else could such a courtroom fixture influence the proceedings? I remember doing a criminal trial in San Bernardino, California. The case was assigned to a new judge who had just spent the past twenty years as a senior prosecutor in the Office of the District Attorney. Within a very short period of time I knew exactly where the Judge stood and she was definitely standing right next to the prosecutor. Can you imagine being the quarterback of a professional team knowing that the referee was going to do everything within his discretion to help the other team win the game?

From the time I first appeared in this courtroom I could see that the court report seemed very friendly and confident and comfortable with the judge during various social exchanges but didn't think anything about it. So the trial commenced and the court reporter seemed to be typing along pretty well without incident. The prosecutor then called the police officer who was obviously a critical witness in this criminal trial and proceeded to elicit his background, training and his observations during this arrest. Things were moving along smoothly and the court reporter looked relaxed and comfortable. That appearance of comfort abruptly ended when it was my opportunity to cross-examine the office about a number of inconsistencies between his testimony and his report. It was a miraculous change because all of the sudden it was as if I was speaking Japanese. As I pointed out the officer's inconsistencies, the court report couldn't seem to understand a word I was saying. I would ask a question such as, "now officer you just testified that you saw the defendant wearing a RED jacket but in your report you wrote that you saw the defendant wearing a BLUE jacket, isn't that true?" The court report would burst out with a SLOW DOWN COUNSEL! Can you repeat that question counsel? I would then repeat the exact same question much slower and so the officer had much more time to gather himself and compose his answer. This went on throughout my entire cross examination so that the officer had the distinct advantage of being able to hear virtually all of my questions twice before answering. After several of these interruptions and outbursts by the court reporter the Judge

17

would then scold me in front of the jury that I was obviously speaking too fast for the court reporter and that she was having trouble recording my questions.

So not only did the court report assist the arresting office on cross-examination by giving him additional time to answer my questions, but the Judge was now scolding me in front of the jury creating the impression that I was somehow doing something improper. Now I didn't have a metronome that day on my desk but I can assure you the rate of my speech was similar that of every other person in the trial.

In addition, since I was asking almost all of my questions twice, the prosecutor had much more time to decide whether to object to the form or substance of the questions. Sure enough, every time the prosecutor would object to one of my questions the judge would sustain the objection which would force me to rephrase my question. So the officer was then answering a tough question he had just heard three times providing the opportunity for a much more composed response.

Who would have thought that a court reporter just typing all of the spoken words in shorthand into a little machine could have such a significant impact on the trial and the jury.

If this court reporter had been assigned to a fair and unbiased judge it is highly unlikely that she would have ever tried to impact the trial the way she chose to do so. And she would have never felt comfortable bursting out at me in front of the jury and telling me to slow down. She would have been quickly replaced by the judge with a different court reporter after her first trial had she pretended to not be able to keep up, or barked at one of the attorneys in front of

18

the jury. It is the judge who allowed and condoned this behavior which effects the juries perception and opinion of the parties, and prejudices the defendants' ability to receive a fair trial.

The Impartial and Omnipotent Judge

Judges preside over the court proceedings. Judges are trained to an extent to exude an aura of confidence. The nature of the position invites them to present themselves as authoritative, willing to listen, but never in doubt about their determinations. Depending upon the case and the personalities involved, the prosecutor and defense might conduct themselves professionally and dispassionately throughout the trial making life easier for the judge. But many times these adversaries become contentious during the trial and can even be outwardly hostile toward each other, forcing the judge to intervene in order to maintain civility and decorum in the courtroom. Judges oversee and facilitate the trial process, make legal rulings, and instruct the jurors on the applicable law.

Curiously, judges in criminal cases are quite often former veteran prosecutors, but it is far less common for a defense attorney to become a judge. The reason for this disparity is due principally to the way in which an attorney becomes a judge.

Generally, to become a local county judge you must either be appointed by the Governor of the state, or be elected to the position in a general election. Federal Judges are appointed by the President of the United States and must be confirmed by a simple majority of the Senate. The Governor is a political animal who looks to appoint well-qualified individuals who are usually from his political party, and less well-qualified supporters, who are politically viable, and will not embarrass the Governor sometime in the future in a high profile case. It also doesn't hurt if you privately agree to support the Governor at the next gubernatorial election.

Being a candidate for judge in an election is a difficult and expensive proposition. A county judicial seat requires a county wide campaign to be successful in a contested election. Speaking engagements at the Rotary Club or Elks Lodge are time consuming. Participating in election debates and media interviews is hard work. Being published in the voter pamphlet materials, putting up hundreds of those silly little signs on every corner, and paying for some advertising, will cost thousands. In a large county, a judicial candidate might spend more than one hundred thousand dollars to successfully run for a contested judicial seat.

The law enforcement community and the local prosecutor's office are by far the most important supporters in a local judicial race. Being tough on crime is a powerful and popular message. Touting your intolerance of abuse by landlords in landlord/tenant eviction cases is not going to garner much support from the voters. If you want to run for a judicial seat, you almost always need the support of your local police and prosecutorial agencies. But how can you garner the support from the police chief and the police unions? You must be tough on crime and promise to support law enforcement if you want support. And what is the surest way to convince the law enforcement community that you are tough on crime and will support them once on the bench? You're a prosecutor trying to become a judge.

Think about the politics behind the process and the

ramifications. What interest could the prosecutor's office and local law enforcement possibly have in the outcome of a local judicial race? If judges are all fair and impartial, who just mechanically decide contested issues based upon the facts and the law, then these groups should really be indifferent as to who becomes a judge. Aren't judges in criminal cases just making legal rulings based upon facts and the applicable law? Why would it matter who is on the bench hearing a case? It turns out that judges have a lot of discretion in the way they handle matters and decide issues and their background and experience impacts their view of those issues.

Judicial candidates spend untold hours telling the community that they will be fair and impartial to all criminal defendants in all cases, while out of the other side of their mouths they proudly boast about being endorsed by every law enforcement union and police chief in the community.
There are obvious reasons which explain why far more judges are former prosecutors than former defense attorneys. As a judge, being fair and impartial usually means something different to a former criminal defense attorney and a former prosecutor.

Judges are often thought of as referees in a sporting event. Can you imagine being in a baseball game where the plate umpire widened the strike zone for the opposing team? Can you imagine being in a football game were all fouls were called on your team but only the most egregious fouls where called on the opposing team? Can you imagine playing in a basketball game. . . you get the point. But haven't we discovered gambling and game fixing by referees in almost every major professional sport? Why would you believe that judicial officers are beyond reproach?

A criminal jury trial is an adversarial process and a presiding judge is supposed to be a neutral and unbiased participant in the process. There are many former prosecutors who have become judges and have been successful in completely abandoning their former allegiance, and they embrace their new role of neutrality. As a veteran jury trial attorney I have appeared before many judges who were formerly veteran prosecutors, but I always knew from past trial experiences with that judge that I was assured a fair trial. It takes a serious effort and deep commitment to make the transition from prosecutor to judge but it can be done, and has been done by many judicial officers.

Likewise, there are times when a criminal defense attorney somehow makes it to the bench and suffers from bias. But fear not! The presiding judge, the judge who assigns judges to particular courtrooms, will swiftly reassign them to civil trials or speeding ticket cases after a few whispers in chambers and complaints from the prosecutors or law enforcement.

Chapter 3: Pre-conviction Proceedings

Justice Delayed is Justice Denied

At the beginning of the trial process the parties appear for trial call in a courtroom and announce to the judge that they are ready for trial. The judge then attempts to assign the case to an available trial courtroom based upon the length of the trial, the type of case, and whatever else concerns the assignment judge.

Courthouses can be busy places. Sometimes there are no courtrooms available to start a trial, and so the assignment judge trails the case to the afternoon, or the following day, or the following week. As long as the defendant agrees to the continuance, the case can be continued to anytime in the future. If the defendant does not agree to the continuance, the case will still be continued, but the length of the continuance is limited by statute, which is usually no more than ten days.

In addition, the trial may be continued for more than ten days over the defendant's objection, if the prosecutor can demonstrate "good cause" for the continuance. Some judges will rule that almost any reason the prosecutor recites is good cause warranting a prosecution request for a continuance of the trial. The Appellate Court has determined that court congestion is not good cause for a continuance, although it is permissible for the judge to trail the trial within the statutory period due to court congestion. The reason for a continuance beyond the statutory period usually comes from the prosecutor.

Here we see another opportunity for judicial discretion to

23

have a chilling effect on the Constitutional right to a jury trial. The judges and the prosecutors are government employees and are paid a salary to be at the courthouse every day. Each continuance requires an appearance by the defense attorney, and the defense attorney must be ready to start the trial at each of those appearances. The process at various courthouses results in trials being delayed for days, weeks, or months. Some judges will even order the defendant to be present for each court appearance. This type of order has a punitive effect and results in the defendant and his or her attorney sitting in the courthouse hallway for dozens of hours, over multiple days, waiting to learn if their trial will start, or be continued again. Most citizens find it difficult to leave work for a jury trial. Almost all citizens are unable to take innumerable days off from work to wait for a trial to commence. This courthouse process puts pressure on citizens to give up their right to a jury trial and either plead guilty or accept a plea bargain which they would not otherwise accept.

In addition, criminal defense attorneys charge money for their services and the more time a trial takes to start and complete, the more money a private defense attorney will need to charge for their services. These increased costs make hiring an attorney for trial very expensive and deters citizens from electing to proceed to trial.

What is the most common reason for court congestion? Unreasonable prosecutors bog down the wheels of justice. When prosecutors do not make reasonable offers to resolve cases, defendants and their attorneys elect to go to trial instead of taking a bad deal because there is a reasonable chance of being acquitted, and even if convicted, the trial judge is likely to sentence the defendant to something less than, or equal to, what the prosecutor was initially offering prior to the trial. This is what causes court congestion.

I remember several years ago in Riverside County, California, when the trial call departments were dismissing a handful of criminal cases each day because the cases had been trailed to the statutory limit, and there were no courtrooms available to commence the trial. The notorious District Attorney refused to modify his tough on crime approach and created a civil backlog for several years because the county court administrators were forced to use civil trial resources to accommodate the unusual criminal case overload. Having civil judges preside over criminal trials is a bad idea for a number of reasons, and most courthouses distinguish between civil and criminal departments.

I should note that many courthouses are very efficient, and the day a case is set for the trial is usually the day you can expect to start the trial, barring something unusual. Also, I have appeared before many assignment judges over the years who have been very flexible about trailing and continuing the case. A judge might tell you that there are no courtrooms available, and then might ask the defense attorney for a preference regarding the next available trial date. Some judges even allow the defense attorney to call the assignment department to check on the daily congestion. I have encountered many very reasonable and accommodating judges who are willing to work through any periods of court congestion. But, this book is about the jury trial process, and the opportunities it presents for judges to impact the outcome of the jury trial. It seems appropriate to illustrate how those same judges can make exercising the right to trial a needlessly time consuming, expensive, and punitive experience.

The Challenges of Trials

Once the case is assigned to a judge, each of the parties usually, depending upon state law, has the right to exercise one challenge to the first judge assigned to them. Trial attorneys are like elephants when it comes to remembering how they were mistreated by a judge in a past trial. Often attorneys will share trial stories about particular judges and the word will spread through the courthouse like a raging wildfire.

But exercising a challenge to a judge is an awkward move because a copy of the paperwork usually makes its way back to the judge you challenge. You do not need to explain the challenge, or make any accusations, but you know that the judge will learn about your challenge. In a smaller courthouse that decision will follow you around for quite some time. High school politics seem so remote from courthouse politics, but I promise you that other judges will also learn which defense attorney challenged a particular judge who might end up being their personal friend or golf buddy. All judges at a courthouse stay connected by meetings, memos, luncheons, and personal relationships. When reelection time comes around every few years for a judge, he or she will look to the other judges at the courthouse for some sort of help or support.

The prosecutor will almost never challenge a judge without the express approval of the top brass in the prosecutor's office. The decision for a prosecutor to challenge a judge is a big deal and can create a political firestorm at the courthouse. When the prosecutors challenge a judge, they effectively remove the judge from hearing criminal trials because no criminal case can be assigned to the judge without a flurry of challenges being filed. Sometimes only one of the many prosecution agencies is challenging a judge, but the other prosecution agencies will still appear before the judge for trial, and so the assignment judge has to consider this factor by looking at the court file to see who filed the criminal charges. Although technically the case should be assigned, allowing the challenge to then be filed, and then the case is reassigned; it doesn't work out that way and no one has the ability to audit the inner thoughts of the assignment judge.

Both parties also have the right to challenge a judge for actual bias and prejudice. If the case involves the burglary of a store, and the judge's wife owns the store, then everyone can agree, without a formal hearing, that the judge should not hear the case. But if you want to hold an evidentiary hearing to argue that the judge is a former veteran prosecutor, and is biased against all criminal defendants, in all criminal cases . . . good luck.

Once a judge is assigned, the prosecutor and the defense attorney make their way to the trial department to check in with the courtroom clerk or bailiff. Sometimes the assignment department clerk or bailiff will take the court file to the trial courtroom, but often the court file is handed to the prosecutor to bring to the trial courtroom. For some peculiar reason, the defense attorney, who is an officer of the court and a member of the state bar, is never entrusted with the court file. This preference seems odd since there are many stories of prosecutors falsifying, hiding, and destroying evidence prior to being terminated for the misconduct. If the trial courtroom is locked and the parties have to wait, the prosecutor has the advantage of being able to peruse the court file for information while waiting for the trial courtroom to be opened by the bailiff.

The Unofficial Meeting

When the parties and the court file find their way to the trial courtroom, the judge will almost always conduct an informal pretrial meeting in the judge's chambers. A chamber sounds impressive but it's just the judge's office which is usually located somewhere off the hallway behind the courtroom. The government building offices are universally unimpressive with the rare exceptions. When you see a beautiful building being used as a courthouse it is often because many of the elected government officials are also located within the building as well. Money and politics are ever-present. Some judges are willing to use the old, grey steel government file cabinets from the 1980's, but some judges pay to furnish their own chambers to spruce up the place.

Smiles and handshakes quickly give way to the business at hand. There are countless ways to conduct a chambers conference and all judges have their own style and personality, but generally, they boil down to the following litany.

"So what's this case all about?" the judge will ask the prosecutor. The prosecutor immediately recites some version of a partially memorized opening statement about the charges and evidence. The judge maintains his best poker face, obviously convinced of complete guilt, and turns to the defense attorney with the next question, "So what's the problem?" The defense attorney politely explains that perhaps not everything the prosecutor told you is completely accurate and we think the evidence at trial will establish innocence. Obviously everything said to the judge will be used by the prosecutor to help him prepare his case, and to better understand the particular defense issues.

"What was the last settlement offer?" the judge asks the prosecutor. "And your client doesn't want to take that deal?" as the judge turns his head and engages the defense attorney. "What is your client interested in?" he asks. "Well, your honor, we would like a dismissal of all the charges and a personal apology from the county prosecutor himself, and a free car wash . . . but barring that, we would be willing to agree to plead guilty to the reduced charge of such and such if the court would agree to a sentence of no more than such and such."

Even if the defendant is completely innocent, it might be prudent to plead guilty to a lesser charge, with an agreed upon a sentence, to avoid the risk that a jury might return a verdict of guilty on the more serious charge, despite his innocence. If convicted, the judge will be forced to impose a sentence in accordance with the sentencing guidelines which pertain to the more serious charge. Although it is rare in my opinion, innocent people are wrongly convicted by juries every single day in the United States and guilty people are acquitted by juries every single day.

When I say wrongful convictions are "rare" what do I mean? Let's say there about 150,000 State and Federal jury trials per year in this country. If the jury gets it right 99% of the time that means that 1% of the time an innocent person is being wrongly convicted because a witness mistakenly identified them, or a prosecution witness lied, or someone hid exculpatory evidence, or something else. That means that 1,500 innocent citizens per year are wrongly convicted. If you place even more trust in our system and believe that the juries get it right 99.9% of the time then you still have to accept that about 150 people per year are wrongly convicted. But what if you have a lifetime of jury experience and you think juries are only accurate about 95% of the time? And what if some of those trials happen to be death penalty cases, or serious felony cases involving decades in prison?

I have a trial story to illustrate the point. Many years ago I had a client who was charged with a misdemeanor hit and run in Los Angeles, California. Let's call him Pablo Escobar for fun because his name turns out to be important to the story. Pablo and his immediate family were sitting around their proverbial crib one Saturday night drinking up a storm and chillaxin. Apparently they were ill-prepared for the booze festival and began runnin low on gin and juice. So Pablo's brother, Hector Escobar, took Pablo's wheels, with or without Pablo's permission, to buy some liquid supplies. Well it turns out, unbeknownst to Hector, that alcohol interferes with the ability to drive a vehicle - who knew? So Hector T-boned another vehicle on the way to the liquor store. Hector, being an honorable man did what any other civic minded person would do, he ran like hell from the scene into the night. Well, the next morning Hector decided to confess to the crime and decided to take responsibility for the accident. Just kidding! The brothers went to the police station to report the car as stolen the night before. The cops were already upset because they knew the vehicle was in an accident the night before and also they knew the real driver was standing before them trying to report it stolen. Despite the pressure from the sergeant and a few threats about filing a false report, the cops were forced to accept the stolen car report. Incidentally, there was no sign of a broken ignition so apparently the well-prepared auto thief had a key.

But this is where the story takes a turn. It turns out that the driver of the vehicle that was hit by Hector did not have auto insurance and her vehicle sustained about seven thousand dollars in damage. If Pablo's car was being driven by Pablo then his insurance company would pay for the repairs. But if the vehicle was stolen and had been driven by an unknown thief who ran off into the night, then Pablo's insurance company would not pay to repair her car.

So the police are sure it's a bogus stolen car report and they bring the victim into the police station for a photo lineup. Generally, a photo lineup is where the cops show a witness or victim several similar looking subjects and ask the person if they can identify the suspect from the photo lineup. The photos can be mug shots from arrests or Department of Motor Vehicle driver license photographs. The police are supposed to follow a specific careful protocol to avoid being suggestive, or to suggest that the suspect is even represented in the photo lineup.

Anyway, somehow she identifies Pablo as the driver. I was never able to figure out if the police helped her, or she did her own detective work to see what he looked like from Facebook, or something else. After the identification, the case was sent to the local County District Attorney, who filed misdemeanor hit and run charges against Pablo.

At the trial I knew that the victim had seven thousand reasons to identify Pablo, but didn't know how she pulled it off. I also knew that Hector was the driver from interviewing several family members. So during the trial, as expected, the victim is asked by the prosecutor if she sees the person who was driving the vehicle that crashed into her and she identified Pablo. I always get a little nervous that they are going to point to me - but she pointed at Pablo.

On cross-examination of the victim I try the standard identification questions but she has been coached by the Deputy District Attorney better than any Superbowl team. The answers are obviously coached.

Q: How far away was the driver?
A: He seemed very close.

Q: Could you clearly see the drivers face?
A: The image is burned into my mind.

Q: How was the lighting?
A: There was plenty of light from every direction, then she recited the location and distance of every light source.

Q: How long did you see him?
A: After the impact he froze and we stared at each other for what seemed like eternity.

Q: Did you speak to the prosecutor about your ability to identify the driver prior to testifying here today?
A: Yes.

Q: Are you aware that if Pablo was the driver you can make a claim against his insurance company?
A: Yes.

Q: But if the driver was an unknown thief you cannot make a claim?
A: Yes.

So the misidentification approach goes absolutely nowhere but I have a plan. I show the victim a picture of Mr. Escobar and ask her to take a long look at the picture of Mr. Escobar. I wait several seconds as she looks at the photo for maximum effect. I ask her if she was absolutely sure that the man in the picture was the man driving the vehicle that night. She tells me she is absolutely sure and there is no doubt about it. She had clearly practiced the answer to that question at least a dozen times in the mirror before the trial.

Then, I call my first witness, momma Escobar, who is the mother of Pablo and Hector. I show her the picture of Mr. Escobar and I ask her if she can identify the man depicted in the picture. Momma Escobar testifies that the man in the picture is her son, Hector. Kaboom! This was one of the best Perry Mason moments I had experienced in years. The judge even flashed a quick smile in my direction.

The witness has now identified both Hector Escobar and Pablo Escobar as the driver. I had successfully established reasonable doubt about guilt. In closing argument I pointed out the misidentification and the fact that the victim had seven thousand reasons to identify Pablo. The prosecutor argued that I somehow unfairly tricked the victim and that she clearly identified Pablo as the driver from the police photo lineup and in the courtroom.

The jury convicted Pablo in just a few hours and the judge put him in jail for ninety days. Hector was the driver of the hit and run vehicle. Should I have appealed? No. The judge was a pleasant, fair, and evenhanded judge who didn't make one legal ruling against me that could possibly form the basis of any appeal. The fact that the jury believed the victim cannot be the basis of any appeal since there was evidence (her identification) that Pablo was the driver. Think about what can happen in a jury trial when a judge intervenes, takes sides, and tries to steer the verdict.

So sometimes cutting a deal in a pre-trial chambers conference can be a smart move even if you are innocent. During plea negotiations the prosecutors control the charges. There is no such thing as judges dismissing charges as part of negotiations without the consent of the prosecutor. Judges can only dismiss charges after a hearing, or trial, when they are making a legal determination about the charges. Judges control sentencing within the sentencing parameters proscribed by the sentencing laws. For example, if a person is sentenced for a burglary charge the sentencing law might mandate that a judge impose something between three and six years. A sentence of two years or seven years would be illegal, and the aggrieved party would appeal the sentence ultimately resulting in a new sentence.

People think that you hire a great lawyer for the courtroom trial, but being a great lawyer starts long before trial and includes the chambers conference, and a lot of deals are reached prior to trial. I have cut many deals in chambers and I have seen quite a few skilled attorneys in chambers negotiate so well that Donald Trump would be envious.

Some judges are not interested in deals. Some judges take the position that all negotiations should have been completed long before the day of trial and as a trial judge their only role is to facilitate the trial. For many, once they hear about the case from the prosecutor they are completely on board and ready to join the team as co-prosecutor. They make it their mission to steer the jury toward the verdict they decided upon when the prosecutor first told them about the case.

Prior Convictions - Back so Soon?

Repeat customers are something that almost every business would aspire to achieve, unless you are a criminal defense attorney. Unfortunately, recidivism rates are high and repeat customers are common.

When a person requests a jury trial in a criminal case, the jury verdict must be unanimous and each juror must be convinced of guilt, according to the legal standard, which is beyond a reasonable doubt. If a person pleads guilty, or is found guilty by the jury, then the judge will impose a sentence. The subject of sentencing can be rather complicated and entire law school courses are dedicated to sentencing laws and issues.

At sentencing, the judge will typically impose a sentence, but then suspend that sentence, place the defendant on probation for a period of time, and impose certain terms and conditions of probation. The judge might alternatively suspend imposition of the sentence, and then place the defendant on probation for a period of time with certain terms and conditions. In the first instance we know the sentence that is imposed and then suspended, but in the second instance the actual sentence remains unknown but can be imposed later on if the defendant does not complete the probationary terms, or violates probation in some way.

For example, let's say a person is charged with selling drugs and the charge carries a maximum sentence of three years in prison. The judge looks at the facts of the case, the defendant's criminal history, and many other factors, and determines that six months in jail is the appropriate punishment. The judge will almost always impose something less than three years or the defendant would have no incentive to plead guilty and would simply choose to fight the case, proceeding to a jury trial no matter how hopeless the case seemed. For example, in a death penalty case there is no such thing as "taking the deal" since the deal is death.

In our example, the judge at sentencing might impose two years in jail, but suspend eighteen months, and place the defendant on probation for five years, with the conditions that he serve six months in jail, attend narcotics anonymous classes, participate in a drug treatment program for six months upon release from jail, and remain law abiding.

What if the defendant hears the proposed sentence and tells the judge, "I ain't doin shit, your honor! My cousin did the drug treatment program and it sucks!" Well, the judge, or his attorney, will explain that the charge allows for a maximum of three years in jail. Therefore, the defendant can agree to either the terms of probation and the six months, or the judge will "max him out" by imposing three years in jail. Life is full of choices.

Once the case is resolved and the sentence is imposed, the matter would now be considered a prior in any subsequent criminal matter. So six months later when the defendant is released from jail, he is arrested again for selling drugs. Actually, the defendant would probably be released in about three months due to jail overcrowding and early release programs but why confuse the story. Anyway, the first arrest is now considered a prior criminal conviction for sentencing considerations by the judge. In addition, because the second arrest occurred within the five years of probation, it will be considered a probation violation if proved.

Here's where things get interesting. The defendant has the right to have a jury trial on the new drug sales charge which must be proven beyond a reasonable doubt. But the probation violation allegation only requires an evidentiary hearing, does not entitle the defendant to a jury, and only needs to be proved by a "preponderance of the evidence" which is generally understood to be "more likely than not" or "51%." Judges almost always find the person in violation of probation using this standard even if the jury finds the person not guilty using the beyond a reasonable doubt standard.

So how do we typically handle such a hearing? The defendant is under a great deal of pressure to settle the new case knowing that the judge has the power to impose a sentence on the probation violation. If the defendant proceeds to trial on the new case and wins, the judge can simply use the trial evidence as the required evidence for the evidentiary hearing on the probation violation and will most likely find the defendant in violation. In our example, the judge could impose another eighteen months for the probation violation since two years was imposed and eighteen months was suspended.

You have the constitutional right to a jury trial in all criminal cases. However, the judge can deny you the right to a jury trial for all practical purposes by exercising his discretion on the sentencing of any probation violation.

If the judge offers nine months for both the new drug sales case and the probation violation on the prior case, what do you think the defendant should do? It's clearly a seller's market and you are basically forced to buy what the judge is selling. If the maximum sentence on the current charge is not significantly longer than the sentencing exposure on the probation violation, then the judge can force you to plead guilty on the new charge by controlling the sentence on the probation violation. Even if you are innocent of the new charges it might be prudent to plead guilty in order to limit your sentencing exposure on the probation violation.

I should probably point out the distinction between jail and prison at this point. Although the terms are often used interchangeably, people involved in the criminal justice system understand the distinctions between jail and prison. Jail is used for short term incarceration by local jurisdictions such as cities and counties. A citizen might be housed in jail awaiting arraignment, trial, sentencing, or serving a sentence, which is usually less than a year. There have been several recent changes in the law which involve housing state prison inmates in local jails, but generally jail is for shorter durations. Strangely, you might have a convicted killer in a local jail waiting for his sentencing hearing where he will be sentenced to prison for the rest of his life, and in the same jail you might also have a mother of two children serving sixty days for stealing money from her employer. Obviously, there is a huge difference between Los Angeles County Jail and a small rural town jail.

Prisons are administered by the states and are used to house convicted criminals for longer durations. Many inmates in prison will never leave the prison and will remain in prison until executed, or will remain in prison for the rest of their lives. Prisons are dangerous places and some refer to prison as gladiator school due to the level of violence and mortal combat. On average, about 160 inmates are killed each year by other inmates, and thousands are seriously injured. In prison, they fight by prison rules. Shoving a pencil through a person's eyeball, or smashing their skull repeatedly into the concrete, would be considered acceptable during a fight under prison rules. Everyone has heard some sort of comment about "prison rapes" and that's because there are about 6,000 prison rapes occurring each year. This number only represents reported rapes. Prison crimes are often unreported because reporting a crime and becoming a "snitch" in prison can get you killed. There are also about 2,000 corrections personnel each year who are injured significantly enough to require medical attention.

When Judges grant probation, and sentence a person to several months in jail as a more lenient sentence than prison, they will often warn the person that an additional offense will result in a sentence to prison. The judge's cautionary warning shows a clear understanding of the difference between jail and prison.

Pretrial Motions

After the pretrial conference concludes, the parties have the opportunity to discuss trial issues and to file any pretrial motions. Motions are used by the parties to settle any anticipated evidentiary disputes outside the presence of the jury before those matters occur in front of the jury.

For example, the prosecutor might disclose a dozen bloody

photos of the victim to the defense attorney. The prosecutor is certainly entitled to show at least one of the photos to the jury to establish his case, but the defense attorney feels that the cumulative effect of all of the bloody photos is too prejudicial, unnecessary, and inflammatory. The defense attorney might file a motion to limit the prosecutor to picking just one bloody photo of the victim. If the defense attorney waited until the jury was present, the prosecutor would display all of the photos in front of the jury, leaving the defense attorney to object in front of the jury, but then it's too late because the jury has already seen the photos in the hands of the prosecutor.

To avoid trial delays the prosecutor might make a motion to introduce certain evidence so that the issue is resolved before the jury is called to the courtroom. This avoids trial objections and trial delays regarding the evidence. It also helps to know what will be allowed into evidence when each party prepares their presentations.

A judge has discretion when allowing or excluding evidence which can have a tremendous impact on the outcome of a jury trial. For example, the jury was never aware that O. J. Simpson received military training with a knife during the filming of a movie in which he starred because this evidence was excluded via a motion. The physical evidence established that the killer of Nicole Simpson and Ronald Goldman was quite skillful with a knife. In this example, the pretrial ruling on the knife training issue appears to have assisted the defense, but pretrial rulings can be devastating to the defense such as allowing the admission of prior criminal convictions or prior bad acts.

Sometimes in the middle of a jury trial the client can

sabotage the entire trial by saying something that allows evidence of his prior convictions to be introduced into the trial although they were already excluded by the judge prior to trial. For example, imagine a defendant being on trial in a driving under the influence case. He takes the stand and proudly declares that he only drank one beer and the cop is full of bologna. On cross-examination the prosecutor asks the defendant about his poor performance on the various field sobriety tests. The defendant quickly blurts out that those tests were too hard, the instructions were too confusing, and he has never done those tests before.

Well it turns out that the defendant has two prior driving under the influence convictions that his brilliant defense attorney skillfully persuaded the judge to exclude from the trial as not relevant to the current driving under the influence charge, and so prejudicial that the defendant would not receive a fair trial from the jury if the jurors became aware of those two prior convictions.

But now the defendant has claimed that his poor performance on the field sobriety tests was due to the instructions being too confusing, and his lack of familiarity with the tests. The prosecutor interrupts the cross-examination and asks for a sidebar. At sidebar the prosecutor argues to the judge that what the defendant said is not true. The defendant has two prior drunk driving convictions and performed field sobriety tests on both of those occasions. Therefore, the defendant is very familiar with the tests and the instructions, which actually would give him a performance advantage on the tests since the tests are designed for the novice with no prior testing experience. The judge agrees and the prosecutor is now allowed to ask the defendant about the two prior arrests and

41

the field sobriety tests on each occasion. This outcome is fair and a fair judge would rule against the defendant and would not allow the defendant to mislead the jury with his untruthful excuse.

It really goes without saying that when a jury hears about the defendant's prior convictions for the exact same charge they are far more likely to convict. Jurors usually do not engage in the mental gymnastics needed to compartmentalize the prior convictions, and to reason that those prior convictions are not really relevant to guilt or innocence of the current charge.

Judges who want to lead a jury toward guilt can successfully use this type of situation to achieve that end. Imagine a similar situation where the defendant is on trial charged with driving under the influence. The defendant takes the stand and proudly declares that he only drank one beer and the cop is full of bologna. Upon cross-examination the defendant is asked why he didn't call a cab. The defendant testifies that he doesn't like to drink and drive and would have called a cab if he believed he was under the influence of alcohol. The prosecutor interrupts the cross-examination and asks for a sidebar. At sidebar the prosecutor argues to the judge that what the defendant said is not true. The defendant does like to drink and drive and has two prior drunk driving convictions to show for it and the prosecutor wants to ask the defendant about those two priors in front of the jury. The defense attorney laughs at the twisted logic and argues that what the defendant said is true. He has suffered the negative consequences of the two prior convictions and does not like to drink and drive, and he only drove because he felt okay to drive. Having the two priors does not demonstrate any affinity for driving under the influence of alcohol. The judge stretches the bounds of logic and imagination and allows the prosecutor to inquire about the two prior convictions which virtually assures a conviction. In the middle of the trial the judge has found a way to sabotage the entire defense.

Some would not be bothered by this ruling because they feel the jury should know everything in order to make their decision. Again, it is difficult for jurors to keep the prior conviction information from influencing their current decision which really has nothing to do with the prior convictions. The rules of evidence which are used throughout the jury trial process are in place to ensure a fair trial. Judges exercise discretion when they make rulings regarding the rules of evidence which can have a devastating impact on the jury verdict.

A judge can lay a trap for the defendant. Before the trial the judge can rule that the evidence of the prior conviction is excluded. Based upon this ruling, a decision is made to have the defendant testify during the trial because the defense attorney knows the defendant cannot be questioned about the prior. Then, in the middle of the trial, while the defendant is testifying, the judge will interrupt the testimony and ask the parties to come forward for a sidebar. At sidebar the judge will advise the parties that based upon the statements of the defendant, he is reconsidering his prior ruling and will now allow evidence relating to the prior conviction. Gotcha!

It turns out that the defendant testified that he was wearing jeans the night of the arrest which he claimed interfered with his ability to stand on one leg and it turns out that the defendant was wearing jeans during both prior arrests. The judge has made a monumental leap in logic to trap the

43

defendant and ensure a conviction.

Behind Closed Doors

CONFIDENTIAL

Some types of hearings are confidential and not open to the public. For example, a mental health/psychological evaluation hearing must be confidential. Or a hearing to view the personnel records of a law enforcement officer would be confidential. If a person arrested reads the arrest report and is appalled at the work of fiction then you might suspect that the officer is a liar. If the officer is a consistent liar then you would expect him to have lied in other matters. So, one thing that can occur is that the defense attorney would file a motion seeking to view the law enforcement officer's personnel records. Now they don't just hand over the officer's personnel file to any defense attorney who has a client moaning about the arresting officer being a liar.

After the defense attorney files the motion seeking records, with proper justification, a hearing is scheduled. The law enforcement agency sends some sort of custodian of records with the personnel file to the hearing. The judge and the custodian of records go into chambers, without the defense attorney, and the judge views all of the records. In this particular instance the judge is supposed to disclose to the defense attorney any citizen complaints, or police discipline, that reasonably relate to dishonesty. If the defense motion involves allegations of excessive force by the arresting officer then the review of the personnel records would be limited to prior incidents or complaints of excessive force by the officer.

Do you see the opportunity for abuse? The judge decides what will be disclosed and you have no way to know whether there was some incident of dishonesty or excessive force that should have been disclosed. Documents and information are discoverable only if the judge orders it to be disclosed. The law enforcement custodian of records is unlikely to tell the defense attorney about the judge exercising his discretion not to disclose a relevant incident and so I have no idea if a judge has ever failed to disclose potentially exculpatory evidence from one of these hearings. Although, based upon the conduct I have observed in open court, I have concerns. You can image how this type of information could affect a jury decision. The judge has tremendous ability to impact the outcome of the trial by stretching his analysis of the disclosure and relevancy of information.

For example, an officer's personnel records might contain a non injury domestic violence incident where police were called to the officer's residence but no arrest was made. However, the police agency took some sort of internal disciplinary action. Of course no arrest was made! He is a police officer and the police officers who responded to the call handled the matter quietly. The disciplinary incident, however, is documented in the personnel file. The judge, who knows he wants to help the prosecutor, rationalizes his decision by telling himself that this incident did not involve the officer while on official duty, did not relate to an arrest, so it is not relevant, and the jury should not be told about it.

45

Therefore, he does not order that it be disclosed to the defense attorney.

But if the charges involve a battery on a police officer and the defense involves the officer's unreasonable use of force, shouldn't the defense attorney be able to bring up the officer's prior violence? Imagine that right after the officer testifies that the defendant attacked him, the defendant testifies that he insulted the officer while intoxicated and the officer then threw him to the ground and punches were exchanged. Could a jury be assisted in determining the truth and reaching a verdict by knowing that the officer attacked his wife previously?

Chapter 4: Courtroom Logistics

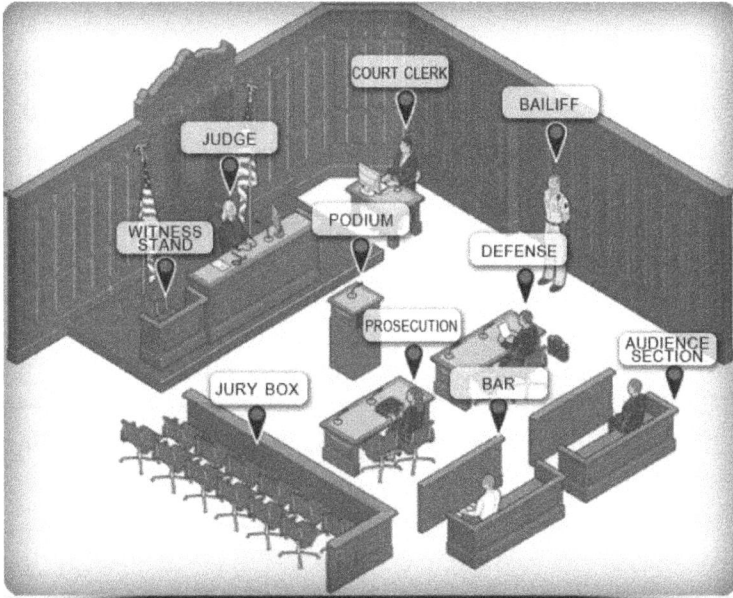

On the Record

Courtroom proceedings are generally recorded so there is a record of the proceedings. The recordings occur with an audio recorder using microphones placed throughout the courtroom or via a court stenographer who feverishly types shorthand into that funny looking typewriter machine. Some courtrooms have neither system in place so all disputes as to what occurred during the trial are reconstructed by each party from memory. Those memories are then submitted via declaration to the appellate court. The trial judge also has the option of submitting his own version of what occurred to the appellate court via a declaration. When an appeal occurs, either party requests that any audio recording be transcribed. The audio is then converted into a transcript, usually by a certified court reporter, which will be submitted to the appellate court.

At times, if the parties and the judge are in agreement, some proceedings are not recorded and are said to be "off the record," for example, chambers conferences or side bars. Side bars are short discussions with the judge during the trial out of the jury's earshot which occur either next to the judge's bench or in the back hallway. Sometimes the parties feel it is necessary to record everything so the court reporter might go into the judge's chambers with the parties to record the communications, or the jury might be asked to leave the courtroom so that the parties can communicate with the judge in open court while the matter is being recorded.

If the judge insists upon everything being on the record it is usually a bad sign. First, the formality and logistics of recording everything takes up extra time and results in the trial lasting longer. More importantly, a judge who insists upon recording everything is a judge who usually has an expectation of being appealed and has usually been through the appellate process more than once. There are exceptions to every rule, but when the judge starts excusing jurors early for lunch so that he can memorialize something on the record for posterity, you just know the judge is all too familiar with being appealed by defense attorneys. There is usually a good reason for the judge to be concerned.

Movies and legal television shows will often make references to matters being "on the record" or "off the record." This is a legal reference to the matter being recorded or not recorded. Journalists have adopted the usage and are known for using the terms "on the record," meaning that the journalist is free to record the matter and disseminate it publicly, or "off the record," meaning that the information is not to be recorded and not to be disseminated.

The "record" consists of just spoken words, and any documents or exhibits admitted into evidence, but communication involves so much more. Books have been written on the subject of body language and nonverbal communication. Words convey the meaning of the speaker but tone, volume, hand gestures, facial expressions, vocal inflections, cadence, and many other nonverbal signals, all combine to convey meaning. In fact, words can mean the exact opposite when used sarcastically. Sure, I believe your story!

Sometimes it can be necessary for the parties to supplement the record with descriptions. For example, a fisherman testifies about a fish he caught. The fisherman testifies that "the fish was this big" which is rather meaningless from the audio recording. So the party examining the witness might say, "Your honor, let the record reflect that the witness is holding his two index fingers approximately thirteen inches apart." The judge who observed the testimony might respond, "the record will so reflect." Now the record has been augmented to give meaning to the physical description by the fisherman.

Another example might be, "Your honor, let the record reflect that you shook your head and rolled your eyes throughout the testimony of the defense alibi witness several times." And the judge might reply, "Request denied! I did no such thing! I'd like to see both counsel in my chambers

49

immediately!"

How about making a motion to place a video camera in the courtroom to record the trial, meaning the unfair judge who keeps rolling his eyes? Denied! However, the courtroom is a public place and is open to the public. The judge can exclude disruptive people, or crying babies, or minors, and there are a few specialized hearings which must be confidential, but generally, the public has the right to observe jury trials. Remember those two little words in the Sixth Amendment, "public trial." So occasionally it becomes necessary to have someone come into the courtroom to observe the trial. The bailiff usually contacts people who enter the courtroom to watch a trial with the pretext of offering assistance, but he usually just wants to see what they are up to. Unbeknownst to anyone in the courtroom, the jury trial enthusiast is actually a paralegal who works for the defense attorney who has been asked to watch the judge throughout the trial. Upon appeal, the trial enthusiast can be called upon to write a declaration detailing their observations of the judge rolling his eyes at all of the defense alibi witnesses.

Incidentally, various organizations like PETA (People for Eating Tasty Animals) in an animal abuse case, or MADD (Mothers Against Drunk Driving) in a high profile driving under the influence case, will occasionally show up to observe jury trials. If their identity in the courtroom audience is unknown, what would be the point to observing the trials? Well, the judge usually knows the organization representatives. Arguably, the activist representative is present to influence the judge, either during the trial or at sentencing. Keep in mind that whether the judge won his seat in a contested election, or was appointed by the

Governor, he will eventually come up for reelection every few years. Most Federal Judges are appointed for life - and for good reason! One reason is to try to avoid politics impacting decisions. Others could argue that we want local judges to be subject to reelection because we want to ensure that the judge's values reflect the community values, and when those values diverge, we want the ability to replace the judge.

Prosecutor Sits Nearest to the Jury

Every real estate agent will tell you that home value is all about location, location, location. The prosecutor sits nearest to the jury.

It is well established that the prosecution always sits at the table closest to the jury. There are no laws mandating this seating assignment, but it seems to be an unwritten rule in every courtroom in which I have appeared. Whenever a defense attorney challenges such custom, the judge or prosecutor typically replies that the government has the burden of proof and is therefore entitled to an added advantage. The fact that the prosecutor chooses to always sit at the table nearest to the jury establishes that this is indeed beneficial.

The judicially sanctioned seating assignment also provides the prosecution with several opportunities. I remember a trial where the defendant had a long and impressive criminal history. I knew all the details because I obtained a copy of his "rap sheet," which most people know from television is a criminal history printout. The prosecution also knew his criminal history and also had a copy of his rap sheet which she conspicuously laid on the corner of her counsel table so it would be visible to all the jurors who were seated just a few feet away from the corner of the table. In addition, the prosecutor left three criminal case file folders on the same corner for viewing by the jury. Each file folder had the prosecution office name stamp and the defendants **NAME** in large, bold block lettering.

When I discovered the unethical tactics, I told the judge and instead of picking a fresh untainted jury we just moved along after he told the prosecutor to quietly put all the objectionable material away and out of view. The judge's remedial efforts not only encourage future misconduct, but left the defendant with a tainted jury.

It may seem odd but the jury is not supposed to know about the defendant's prior criminal history unless it has some logical relevancy to the current charge. For example, if the defendant is charged with being the aggressor in a fight, then it might be fair to allow the jury to know that the defendant has been previously convicted twice of starting fights. Generally, prior criminal conduct is not admissible and is very prejudicial because a jury will be heavily influenced by the prior conduct although logically it usually has no relevancy as to whether the defendant is guilty of the current criminal charge.

Often the prosecutor will have the arresting officer sitting beside them for a portion of the trial. This also provides the prosecutor and law enforcement officer an opportunity to intentionally whisper so loudly that jurors can overhear them. Virtually any prejudicial thing can be said. Can you imagine the devastating impact on a juror from overhearing the prosecutor whispering to the officer that the defendant told the same story in his last trial, or overhearing that the defendant was going to plead guilty if we agreed to twenty years but we demanded thirty years and so he chose to try his luck at trial? The seating assignment used by the judge creates a general advantage for the prosecution and creates a number of powerful opportunities.

Not only does the prosecutor sit at the table closest to the jury, but in some courthouses the prosecutor sits first. The most common custom that I have experienced is that both the prosecutor and the defense attorney sit in the hallway and wait for the bailiff to open the door each morning and after the lunch hour recess. The jurors then remain outside while both attorneys enter the courtroom and begin trial preparations. Attorneys might ask to speak to the judge about a matter, or might need to check with the clerk about exhibits, or might need to set up a projector or video or any other logistical task necessary to present the case smoothly to the jury.

In a few courthouses the prosecutor is treated differently which arguably makes the jurors think about them differently. Some courthouses have courtrooms with access via keyless coded door locks or swipe card lock systems. For some reason the prosecutors are given access, but the defense attorneys are not. Therefore, every day during the trial the prosecutor authoritatively enters the courtroom while the defense attorney sits in the hallway with the jurors. The prosecutor has the logistical advantage of being able to prepare while the defense attorney waits outside. The prosecutor can communicate confidentially with the courtroom clerk and bailiff about his intentions regarding witnesses or the need for exhibits. After the prosecutor has completed his preparations, the bailiff will open the door and will let the defense attorney, his client, and the jurors enter. The defense attorney has to scramble to set up and might slide over to the clerk to check on something which the prosecutors will be able to eavesdrop upon. But there are more important advantages than allowing the prosecutor to set up while the defense attorney scrambles around haphazardly to gather his trial notes and documents.

The courtroom access suggests to an observant juror that the prosecutor is more like a trusted staff member, similar to the courtroom clerk and the bailiff, and the defense attorney is not. As the jurors and the defense attorney enter the courtroom the prosecutor appears composed, well prepared, authoritative, and he makes eye contact with the jurors and is able to read body language while the defense attorney is kept busy with his preparations. Treating the attorneys differently allows the jurors to view them differently. Both attorneys are members of the state bar, court officers, and are supposed to be equally trustworthy.

Bailiff Watches the Defendant

The bailiff would have you believe that at any moment an armed gunman might burst into the courtroom blasting indiscriminately at any target of opportunity. The courtroom bailiff is responsible for the security of the courtroom and so the judge gives the bailiff great latitude in that regard. Moving around the courtroom might have a tactical advantage in terms of bad guys not knowing exactly where the bailiff is located within the courtroom. Many bailiffs have former military experience and are more than eager and ready to respond to any tactical situation. This tactical security need is used to justify the bailiff engaging in a wide range of behaviors. Therefore, all communications between the defense attorney and the defendant must be whispered because the bailiff can eavesdrop upon the conversation and could then secretly tell the prosecutor what he overheard which might give the prosecutor a massive tactical advantage depending upon the content. All written materials should be concealed inside trial notebooks so that the notebook can be closed when the bailiff stands behind you, and all written materials and documents should be placed face down on the defense table. This is to avoid the bailiff reading all of your confidential notes and documents and then secretly telling the prosecutor at the first recess in the trial.

Isn't that illegal, or unconstitutional, or just plain not right, or something? The judge has some version of a carefully crafted answer for you. Sir, the bailiff is in charge of courtroom security and it is his duty to protect us, and he has great latitude to effectuate his job. Officer Friendly is a decorated war hero who has served his country proudly and has been my courtroom bailiff for the past decade, and if he has any concerns regarding the security of this courtroom then it is his job to pursue those concerns to safeguard us all. It is the responsibility of both attorneys to protect their written and verbal communications and not to allow anyone to hear or see something they wish to remain private.

But now the prosecutor knows the trial strategy and knows about our defense. Another cumulative advantage for the prosecutor has been achieved by the judge's courtroom staff. Can you imagine the batter in a baseball game knowing whether the next pitch will be a ball or a strike? Can you imagine a football team knowing the next play? The New England Patriots knew their opponent's plays, so why should we be shocked and surprised about the prosecutor secretly learning the strategy of the defense attorney in a local jury trial?

Chapter 5: Voir Dire for Cause

The term *voir dire* is a Latin word that generally means to speak the truth. In the course of a criminal trial when prospective jurors are initially called into the courtroom, they are asked to participate in the *voir dire* process. During the *voir dire* process the attorneys are given a brief opportunity to ask each prospective juror questions regarding the appropriateness of having them serve as a juror in the particular case. This initial courtroom experience is an ideal opportunity for the judge to start shaping those young impressionable minds toward a verdict of his choosing with a variety of finely honed techniques.

It is critical to understand the *voir dire* process in order to understand how a judge can subtly and skillfully manipulate the process.

There are a number of significant rules regarding the questioning process that are not disclosed to the prospective jurors. First, the judge will set a time limit for each attorney to ask questions so juror filibusters and follow ups must all be strategically considered. In addition, the questions must be somehow related to a subsequent "challenge for cause" by either attorney. What this means is that after the questioning of the jurors is complete, each attorney will have an opportunity to challenge a juror for cause. In effect, the attorney is asking the judge to remove the juror from the prospective panel because the juror does not appear capable of rendering a fair and impartial verdict based upon the information they provided during the *voir dire* process. The judge will either grant or deny the request. The judge will also have the option of asking questions and interacting with the jurors at his discretion. Most of the time the judge will start the ball rolling, prior to the attorneys, by asking some general questions about employment, prior jury service, area of residence, and whether they know any of the parties or potential witnesses.

After the challenges for cause have been resolved, each attorney then has an opportunity to exercise peremptory challenges. Peremptory challenges provide each attorney the right to dismiss any juror at their discretion, with a limit of usually ten in criminal cases. There are some obvious limitations to that discretion, for example, an attorney is not allowed to try to excuse all the minorities, or women, or some other protected class. But, the prosecutor can surely kick anyone off the jury who has been arrested, and the defense attorney can surely kick anyone off the jury who is related to law enforcement.

What happens if an attorney uses all ten peremptory challenges and is still very unhappy with the jury as constituted? Tough! This is the jury that will decide your case.

As each attorney asks questions, they of course have many objectives in mind. The attorneys want to establish some credibility with jurors. They want to establish some rapport. They want to generally ingratiate themselves with the jurors. And they would like to prejudice the jurors in their favor, although this is not permitted.

The prosecution oriented judges are all well known to the prosecutors from prior trial experiences which have been shared among the prosecutors. So when the case is being heard by one of these judges, the prosecutors may try to push the limits with questions that could not possibly relate to a challenge for cause with the only intention being to prejudice the jurors in their favor. Defense counsel will of course object, and the judge will overrule the objection and will allow the question to be asked to the juror. This is an easy way for the judge to allow the prosecutor to unduly prejudice the jurors against the defense.

A Shooting in the Courtroom

For example, the prosecutor might appropriately ask a prospective juror if they agreed with the defendant having a right to a jury trial. This appears appropriate enough because if you don't accept the defendant having a right to a trial by jury then you can't follow the law that allows this right, and can't be a fair and impartial juror and should be excused. But then the prosecutor will follow up with the same juror and will tell the juror that the defendant could jump out of his chair right this minute, and he could grab the bailiff's gun and shoot him and kill him right in front of all of us. And with a courtroom of witnesses to the shooting and his guilt undeniable, he would be entitled to enter a not guilty plea and demand a jury trial. Would that also be okay Mr. Juror? OBJECTION YOUR HONOR!, screamed the defense attorney. Your honor, that question is highly prejudicial, is not really a question but is merely prejudicial argument, and is not intended to be a question related to a challenge for cause. In a very dismissive and annoyed voice the judge declares, "Overruled. I will allow it."

This is just one of an infinite number of examples of how a judge in the adversarial process allows the prosecution to taint the jurors with prejudicial information. The prosecutor's question is a charade and the bogus question is intended solely to suggest that just because we are about to commence a trial does not in any way mean that there is any real doubt about the defendants undeniable guilt. I have heard this question asked several times in the same county because the top brass in the prosecutor's office developed this question and incorporated it into their training program, and several of the judges in the county allow the question over defense objections.

Before hearing any evidence or facts, jurors are now thinking about the possibility that this whole trial might just be a total waste of time and there might not be any legitimate defense at all.

Rehab for Jurors

Rehabilitation is another tool that can be used by judges to impact the trial by stacking the jury against the defense. A defense attorney might spend a few precious minutes with a prospective juror trying to establish that the juror cannot be fair and impartial. Nobody wants to believe that they are incapable of being fair so getting a prospective juror to admit this requires years of experience and great communication skills. Remember that the judge imposed time limits on the process, so time spent with the one juror is time not spent trying to evaluate other jurors.

The defense attorney starts out slow and speaks softly. He asks juror #7 about his law enforcement family which she mentioned in response to the judge's initial general background questions.

Q: Now Juror #7 you said that your father was a police officer?
A: Yes.

Q: And your grandfather was a police officer?
A: Yes.

Q: And your son is a police officer?
A: Yes.

Q: Now this is a criminal case where a police officer will testify. This courthouse is filled with all sorts of civil cases with people arguing about money. Don't you agree with your family being in law enforcement that it might be difficult for you to be fair and impartial in this type of criminal case?
A: Yes. I guess you're right.

Q: I can assure you ma'am that we can send you right down the hallway and you can hear a civil case. Do you think that would be okay with you?
A: Yeah I guess you are right.

Q: If you decided you didn't believe the officer in this case and voted not guilty do you think that might make you feel uncomfortable if you told your relatives?
A: Probably.

Q: Thank you ma'am for your honesty. We will see what we can do about finding you a civil case down the hall that does not involve a law enforcement officer okay?
A: Okay.

Q: Juror #9 Do you think . . .

It is obvious that juror #7 should not be on this jury and that she could not be completely fair and impartial. However, the judge now exercises his discretion to try to rehabilitate juror #7 so that she remains on the jury and forces the defense attorney to use one of the ten important challenges. A challenge used on a juror such as this is a challenge that could have been used on another juror who turns out to be the wife of the police chief.

The judge asks the following questions to juror #7:

Q: Now juror #7 you said you have several members of your family in law enforcement and that through them you know several officers. But you don't personally know the officer who will testify in this case, Officer Smith?
A: No, I don't know him.

Q: And could you listen to his testimony and make up your own mind about his truthfulness?
A: Yes I could do that.

Q: So can you tell me any specific reason why you could not be totally fair and impartial as a juror in this trial?
A: Uhmm. No, I can't think of any specific reason right now.

Q: So you could be fair and impartial? The judge is smiling and nodding his head up and down like a bobble head as he asks the question almost begging juror #7 to affirm his statement.
A: Uhmm. Yes.

Later in the hallway, outside the presence of the jurors, the judge will deny the request to excuse juror #7 for cause because she said she could be fair and impartial. Those are the magic words.

A prospective juror can be in a wheel chair, paralyzed by a drunk driver, and as long as they claim they can be fair and impartial, the judge can legally justify keeping them as a juror in a driving under the influence of alcohol case.

However, the same judge can excuse a prospective juror with an obvious bias against the prosecution who claims to be fair and impartial. The judge might say that the person said they could be fair but didn't say the word impartial. Or the judge might say that the person used the words fair and impartial but I don't believe they are being honest with us and will grant the prosecutors challenge for cause.

Sometimes a judge, with years of trial experience, will even solicit a rookie prosecutor for a challenge for cause about a specific prospective juror by telling the newbie prosecutor that due to a juror's statement he would entertain a motion to excuse that juror by either party. The statement was that the juror hated all cops but he could put it all behind him for this trial. Obviously the judge is talking to the prosecutor when he disingenuously says he would entertain a motion to dismiss the juror from "either side."

Chapter 6: The Witnesses

Witnesses are an essential part of any criminal prosecution. Witnesses testify regarding information needed to establish the violation of the criminal charges. Various governmental agencies prosecute criminal matters. A criminal case might be filed against a citizen by the local City Attorney, County District Attorney, State Attorney General, or United States Attorney General.

Whichever governmental agency brings charges, the prosecution of criminal cases always involves witnesses called by the prosecutor. In criminal matters, those witnesses are usually law enforcement officers of some variety. A criminal case might involve a local city police officer, county sheriff, state agent, a federal officer or agent. There are around one million law enforcement officers employed in the United States depending upon whether you include all law enforcement employees or just sworn officers.

Most law enforcement officers receive some training in courtroom presentation. The training varies widely, but generally, the idea is to familiarize the officers and agents with the courtroom process, etiquette, and some basic rules of the courtroom. One of the benefits of this training is to create a more confident witness who exhibits professionalism and appears to be a more credible witness. Jurors are watching and listening to all of the witnesses and they must determine credibility and accuracy, and this fact is not lost upon law enforcement agencies who train their employees in order to create polished witnesses.

Professional law enforcement witnesses are generally a good

thing, but they can also be disastrous to the fair outcome of a case when jurors mistakenly place too much weight upon their polished testimony. It is quite normal for a juror to compare and contrast all of the witnesses, and to disbelieve or discount the testimony of a witness who has had no courtroom training and appears nervous and unpolished.

I have had many experiences in trial with many different law enforcement witnesses. I have observed brand-new officers do a fantastic job while on direct and cross-examination. I have also seen veteran officers who couldn't remember most of the details of the arrest and had to refer to their police report every other question to read the answer. This creates a bad impression of the officer for the jury.

Some officers really just want to be honest and will answer almost anything as fairly and accurately as possible, even if the answer is unfavorable to the prosecutor. They just want to be honest and don't want to risk being caught in a lie which can have serious consequences for their career.

Some officers are defiant and think every question from the defense attorney is a trick. If you ask them their name, you can actually watch them pause before they answer to avoid any careless mistakes. I do not have the ability to read minds, but I do have the ability to read people, and when I ask some officers their name I swear I think the officer is thinking it's a trick question.

First Impressions

Judges have tremendous flexibility when they use nonverbal communication in the courtroom because generally only verbal communication is recorded throughout the trial for appellate purposes. Imagine this scenario. The prosecution calls a police officer to the stand. The judge's face lights up like a boy on Christmas morning gazing at the presents under the tree for the first time. In a soft friendly tone the judge enthusiastically declares, "Welcome Officer Jones" as if he were greeting a dear old friend into his home. The smile on the judge's face never fades like a beauty pageant contestant posing on the stage. The judge motions with his hand toward the open witness seat and invites the officer to move toward the seat by saying, "please step forward and have a seat in the witness box." From the tone of the invitation you might mistakenly think it was an exclusive courtroom VIP seat reserved for dignitaries only. The jury watches the entire interaction between the judge and the Officer and can only assume that they are longtime friends and that the judge has the ultimate respect and admiration for this fine law enforcement officer so nobly protecting and serving the community. The judge graciously points out the water in a pitcher directly in front of the officer and asks the prosecutor to proceed whenever he is ready.

Defendant's Special Welcome

When the defendant chooses to testify on his own behalf, the greeting from the judge is quite different. The judge stares suspiciously at the Defendant for an uncomfortable extra second or two as the intimidated defendant visibly gulps and squirms a bit. "Welcome Mr. Defendant," the judge declares in a slow, calm, deep tone. "Please step forward and have a seat in the witness box," the judge commands. From the seriousness of the moment an onlooker might mistakenly conclude that some sort of execution was immanent. The judge appears almost distressed by the surprise witness announcement as he grabs a pen and notepad to record anything the witness might say. After being seated the judge insists that the defendant speak directly into the microphone which is positioned exactly where the officer left it after his testimony. "Now pull that microphone toward you as far forward as it will move and slide forward in the chair so that we hear every word," he tells the witness. The acoustics are very poor in this courtroom he disingenuously claims. As the defendant starts his testimony by stating and spelling his name for the record his voice blasts through the courtroom speaker system and echos like a football stadium announcement. The volume is startling and is nearly twice as loud as when the officer testified which continues to unsettle the witness. As the defendant jumps back from the microphone, the judge commands him to lean forward and continue. As he testifies, the judge frantically writes on his notepad and stares at him which is all being observed by jurors who subconsciously start taking far more notes. As the witness testifies, he sees the judge in his peripheral vision next to him staring at him and repeatedly turns toward the judge making increasingly awkward eye contact. The judge can be seen occasionally shaking his head back and forth in disagreement and rolling his eyes as the witness directly contradicts the officer's recollection of events. It is clear to any observer that the judge has already determined who is more accurate and truthful, but the judge will later instruct the jurors on the record that they alone must determine truthfulness and accuracy.

The transcript of both scenarios will read almost identically. In the first scenario the judge said, "Welcome Officer Jones, please step forward and have a seat in the witness box." In the second scenario the judge said, "Welcome Mr. Defendant, please step forward and have a seat in the witness box. Now pull that microphone toward you as far forward as it will move and slide forward in the chair so that we hear every word." Using the appellate standard, the Court of Appeals could not possibly conclude anything was unfair.

A judge can also intervene when the defense attorney uses an expert at trial. There are many criminal cases which require one or both of the parties to use an expert. Cases can involve many fields requiring expert testimony including: ballistics, fingerprints, DNA, police policy and procedure, or drugs. An expert is very loosely defined as someone who has special skill, knowledge, or training in a particular field. Most people mistakenly believe that an expert must have an advanced degree from a prestigious university, or must be world renowned and recognized by everyone in their field. However, a local mechanic could be called to testify as an expert regarding the mechanical operation of brakes. A police officer who is an instructor at the police academy could be called as an expert in police procedures and the proper use of force. A jeweler could be called to testify as an expert on the value of some stolen jewels.

When a party calls an expert to the stand there are certain formalities which typically must be followed, unless the parties stipulate to the witnesses' expertise, which rarely occurs. Before an expert expresses their opinion, or provides information, their expertise must be established. So, the party calling the offered expert will run through a script where the witness describes their background, credentials, and experience, which would qualify them as an expert. It is rare that the party calling the witness would stipulate to the witness being an expert because it is desirable to allow the jury to hear all of the witnesses' qualifications and credentials in order to give their opinion greater credibility and weight. If the opposing party does not believe the person is qualified as an expert they can challenge the witness and the judge will give them an opportunity to ask a limited number of questions to try to establish their lack of qualifications. This is rarely tried because, as I mentioned, qualifying as an expert is rather easy and a party is unlikely to mistakenly call a chemical engineer to testify as to why a bridge collapsed which would require a civil engineer, or a mechanical engineer. After the expert foundation has been accomplished, the party calling the witness will proceed to elicit the desired information and opinions.

After the expert expresses an opinion the expert is subject to cross-examination where the opposing party will challenge their opinion in a variety of ways. The cross-examination might involve challenging their education, or their limited experience, or their affiliation with the prosecution or defense, or their lack of field experiments, or some other approach.

Most experts testify frequently and become known around the courthouse. Once an expert testifies, they establish a record because most trials are recorded. If you want to know what an expert will say in a particular type of case just track down when they last testified and order the audio tape of their testimony for a few dollars. If the expert develops a reputation of changing their opinion to accommodate the party using their services, then it might be prudent to have the audio transcribed in order to confront them with it when they say something totally different. Most local courthouse rules require a transcript because it can be so difficult to play the audio recording repeatedly, and their can be disagreement over what was actually said if the recording is garbled or inaudible.

This transcript only policy also makes it more difficult, time consuming, and expensive for the defendant to challenge any of the usual prosecution experts since transcripts are expensive and take time to prepare. The prosecutors are usually not concerned about trial costs since the government pays the bill. In fact, why not bring in two experts if there is a plausible need and the testimony is not cumulative.

Judges on the bench see the same experts again and again, and hear the same type of testimony over and over. They also hear the same type of cross-examination of the various experts. The prosecutors' office will keep files on each expert regularly used by the defense attorneys and the files are available for each prosecutor to review.

A judge can dramatically undermine the opinion of the defense expert by choosing to ask questions which challenge the witnesses expertise. For example, imagine that the prosecutor calls an expert from the F.B.I. laboratory. The witness describes his education, his employment with the F.B.I., and his experience with ballistics. The witness then testifies that the gun found in the defendant's home was the gun used to kill the victim. Then the defense calls their expert to the stand. The expert describes his education, his former employment with the F.B.I., and current employment as a ballistics expert consultant, and his experience with ballistics. Before the defense attorney can ask him about his opinions, the judge interrupts. The judge begins to ask the defense expert a series of questions which have evolved from watching other prosecutors unsuccessfully attempt to challenge the witness. The questions include the following:

Q: Now Mr. Defense expert, you said you worked for the

F.B.I in the ballistics department, but isn't it true that you spent most of your time in the fingerprint department?

A: Yes, your honor.

Q: And you only spent the last three years of your employment in the ballistics department before retiring, is that right?

A: Yes. I spent several years in fingerprints before transferring to ballistics.

Q: Now when you retired you did so with a pending discipline accusation against you, isn't that correct?

A: Yes, your honor. I had a poor relationship with a supervisor who reported me for preparing inaccurate reports. Rather than spend a year fighting the discipline charges, and continuing to work for the supervisor who was going to demote me, I chose to retire.

Q: And you have not worked for the F.B.I. for the past several years and so you have not read the most recent top-secret ballistics reports available only to F.B.I. experts?

A: Yes, your honor. Those annual ballistic studies cost the F.B.I. millions to prepare and the F.B.I refuses to disclose them to private ballistic consultants specifically so that the F.B.I. experts can pretend to be a more qualified expert. However, I have read every published ballistic study in the last decade.

Alrighty then! Counsel, you may proceed. The defense attorney now asks the expert about the gun and the expert expresses the opinion that the gun found in the defendant's home was not the gun used to kill the victim. The opinion has been undermined by the judge and the jury is sure to give it less weight and credibility.

Some judges will try to find a way to preclude the testimony of the defense expert. Preventing the defense expert from testifying can have a profound impact on the outcome of a jury trial. In our ballistic example, the jury would be left with only the opinion of the prosecution expert that the gun found in the defendant's home was the gun used to kill the victim.

Let me explain how a judge might try to exclude testimony from the defense expert. Imagine a drug case where the defendant has been charged with being under the influence of heroin. Subsequent to her arrest, the defendant was taken to the police station and her blood was drawn for analysis. The blood sample was stored at the police station and was later transported to the county regional crime lab for analysis using gas chromatography-mass spectrometry.

Most counties and cities buy almost everything using the lowest bid criteria, and lab equipment is no exception. The county typically buys the cheapest machines and usually replaces them after several years, when they start to develop maintenance issues. There are several manufacturers of gas chromatography (GC) machines, and each manufacturer usually makes several models, but they all work on the same scientific principles. These machines are complicated, but the testing method can be understood with a little effort and interest.

Governmental agencies purchase far more machines than private laboratories, and so the manufacturers will often cater to any requests from the bulk buyers. One request might be that a manufacturer does not release any of the ownership, maintenance, or performance information about their machines to anyone unless they purchase a machine. Some manufacturers will even agree to sell their machines only to law enforcement crime labs.

Why in the world would various local and regional law enforcement crime labs seek to establish such policies? These "lab protocols" will make it difficult, or impossible, for criminal defense attorneys to find qualified experts who would testify about the substandard lowest bid machines, and the lack of expensive safeguards, and the lack of expensive internal quality control standards and the lack of maintenance per the manufacturer, and all sorts of other deficiencies. The policy not only artificially safeguards the reputation of the machine, but it makes it easier for crime lab employees to testify about the machines and results without any rebuttal from a defense expert.

Even if a judge allows a defense expert to testify regarding the machine, the prosecutor will simply cross-examine the defense expert regarding their lack of familiarity with the specific machine. Of course this lack of familiarity is intentionally created by the law enforcement crime labs themselves, and the manufacturers. This policy benefits the crime labs by helping them to win the battle of the experts, and it helps the manufacturers by avoiding having their machines bad mouthed by defense experts.

Prior to trial the prosecutor would normally disclose their crime lab results and crime lab witness. Similarly, the defense attorney would disclose the name of a defense expert. The prosecutor knows from reviewing the crime lab documents that the lab used the Perfectmachine GC2100, and knows the manufacturer's confidentiality policy which keeps machines and information away from anyone not employed by a law enforcement lab. Therefore, the prosecutor objects to the defense expert and tells the judge that the defense expert lacks the qualifications to express an opinion about the machine. The judge asks a few questions and schedules an evidentiary hearing outside the presence of the jury.

These types of hearings are expensive to the defense and drive up trial costs, because now the defense expert has to be paid twice to come to court to testify about the machines. These types of additional costs have a chilling effect on citizens choosing to exercise their right to trial by jury.

At the evidentiary hearing, the defense expert might testify to having worked in a law enforcement crime lab for twenty years before establishing their own private lab. The expert will have all of the requisite educational background and experience, but will never have used a Perfectmachine GC2100 which is only sold to law enforcement crime labs. The expert has used many GC machines in his career, and owns a Perfectmachine GC2000, but has never used a Perfectmachine GC2100. The GC2000 is nearly identical to the GC2100, except the GC2000 is for single sample analysis, and the GC2100 is a high-volume machine which is capable of testing up to 100 samples per test run, making it desirable for a busy regional crime lab. In addition, the expert has never read the owners manual, repair manual, or performance information for the GC2100 which is not available from the manufacturer, at the request of law enforcement. The expert explains that the internal workings of the Perfectmachine GC2100 are the same as many other machines which he has used and owns, and explains how the basic science of these machines has not changed in the past forty years.

Based upon the hearing testimony, the judge exercises his discretion and refuses to allow the defense expert to testify about the Perfectmachine GC2100, and the crime lab results. The judge has become an accomplice to the system orchestrated by the law enforcement labs, which is designed to present unimpeachable results. In order to testify in a particular case, some judges would require the defense expert to purchase each machine used in each case, in order to testify regarding the machine deficiencies. Obviously, this is not economically viable for an expert to buy every machine on the market, and some manufacturers will not even sell equipment to private labs.

The judge has exercised his discretion to help the prosecutor win the war in the battle of the experts by precluding defense expert testimony regarding the machine used to test the defendant's blood. In criminal cases there are many types of machines, and many types of tests. You can see how a judge can use the same flawed analysis to exclude expert testimony in cases involving ballistics, fingerprints, DNA, police policy and procedure, drugs, or virtually any area requiring expert testimony. The jury would never know that the defense disputes the results, and wanted to challenge the validity of the test results.

Sometimes law enforcement create their own experts so that they can testify in court as an expert. You should trust the officer because he is an expert. How do you know a particular officer is an expert in something? The officer went to expert school, taught or arranged by law enforcement, and at the end of the training everyone receives a certificate indicating they are an expert.

For example, police frequently arrest people who are under the influence of drugs. It can be difficult to prove a person is under the influence of drugs because people react differently to different drugs and exhibit various behaviors and symptoms. So, law enforcement sends officers to several hours of drug recognition classes. The training can be pretty silly and is fairly simplistic. In the training they tell officers that drugs can produce both erratic and calm behavior. Drugs can cause emotions such as crying and depression, or happiness and laughter. Basically, the officer will be taught that almost any behavior could be consistent with drug use. At the end of the classes all the officers receive Drug Recognition Expert (DRE) certificates. Now the officer can come to court and tell the jury they are a drug recognition expert, and in their opinion, the defendant was under the influence of drugs based upon their crying, or laughter, or sadness, or happiness.

Why not just do a chemical test? Most drugs are detectable in the blood for a period of time, and so you can prove a person used drugs "recently," within the past few days or weeks, but you cannot establish exactly when they used drugs. The DRE is needed to testify that the person was under the influence of drugs at the time of arrest.

Let me share a DRE story. I represented a young man who was charged with driving under the influence of marijuana. The young man fell asleep behind the wheel while waiting in a fast food drive-thru line at 2:00a.m.. The restaurant called the police and the police woke him up several minutes later. He explained to the police that he just got off work and was very tired. The police suspected he was drunk and so they had him perform field sobriety tests but he performed fairly well. However, not to be deterred, they gave him an alcohol test and the results were negative - zero alcohol. Then they asked him about drugs and he admitted that he smoked marijuana frequently and last smoked the day before. The police arrested him for driving under the influence of marijuana and took him to jail. A little later a veteran officer who was a certified DRE came to the jail and did an evaluation of my client and wrote a report indicating that my client was basically "wasted." The report described the gross motor impairment and detailed every possible symptom associated with marijuana use. The officer added a few comments about my client giggling and having the "munchies", and even claimed to have observed marijuana stems and leaves in his mouth.

The lab results confirmed that my client had marijuana in his system, but these tests only establish that he had used marijuana within the past several days or weeks. Remember that my client told the police he used marijuana the day before his arrest, but denied smoking anything the night of the arrest.

At trial the DRE officer testified to being a Drug Recognition Expert, described the obviously intoxicated defendant, and expressed the expert opinion that my client was under the influence of marijuana for driving purposes. I asked the officer only two questions on cross-examination and sat down. Two questions I knew from my own self taught expertise would prove the officer was a big fat liar. What two questions did I ask the officer?

I asked the officer how long the physical and psychoactive effects of marijuana last. The officer responded correctly indicating that depending upon experience, frequency of use, and potency, marijuana will generally affect a person for 2-3 hours. I next asked the officer the time of his evaluation of my client. The officer reviewed his report briefly and indicated that he conducted his drug evaluation at the jail at 6:34a.m..

The DRE officer was totally unaware that the defendant had been sitting at the jail since 2:30a.m. when the officer arrived for the evaluation. Prior to that, the defendant had been observed sleeping by the fast food employees since 2:00a.m.. The client could not have used marijuana at any time after 2:00a.m. which means the DRE officer was conducting his evaluation at least four hours and thirty-four minutes later. Since the effects of marijuana last 2-3 hours, the jury knew the DRE officer was exaggerating about his evaluation and observations. In addition, the field sobriety test performance at about 2:15a.m. by a different officer was inconsistent and irreconcilable with the drug evaluation and observations.

It's disturbing how many officers will routinely write arrest reports about observing a white powder around the defendant's nostril during a under the influence of cocaine arrest. But what happens later on when the lab results are negative and no drugs are detected? The prosecutors quietly reject these cases, throw the police reports in the trash, and decline to file charges. Are officers ever held accountable for bogus "stems and leaves in the mouth" observations, or "white powder around the nostrils" observations? No. Most of the time citizens are so relieved that charges were not filed against them that they have no interest in filing a complaint about the officer with the law enforcement agency. However, the prosecutors who are responsible for filing criminal complaints read these exaggerated arrest reports from the same officers regularly, and the liars are easily identifiable, but for some reason the prosecutors rarely take an interest in pursuing the fictional report writers. Keep in mind that when the lab results are positive because of "recent" drug use, and charges are filed, these same officers will testify falsely in court, under penalty of perjury, about these fictional observations. But this courtroom perjury does not seem to motivate most prosecutors to weed out the dishonest officers.

Officer Friendly Protected on Cross-Examination

For some judges, when a law enforcement officer takes the stand at trial that officer is automatically enrolled in the Witness Protection Program. The judge will say or do almost anything to protect the Officer from impeachment on cross-examination.

In a trial, the party calling a witness examines the witness by asking him or her about facts and information. After the examination of a witness, the opposing party has an opportunity to ask the witness questions about that testimony, or some other related matter, during cross-examination.

John H. Wigmore was a well-known trial attorney and legal scholar who is famously quoted as saying that cross-examination is the greatest legal engine ever invented for the discovery of truth.

Witnesses usually come to court well prepared and well rehearsed with a story to tell. But it is the cross-examination that reveals the truth, the whole truth, and nothing but the truth.

All of us have experienced an informal type of cross-examination in our daily lives. An employee arrives at work late with a carefully crafted tale about being late due to his car breaking down. You ask the employee what happened? Where did his car break down? Where was the car taken? Which tow service did you use? What is the estimate for the repair? Where is the tow receipt? Why didn't the employee call in to work to let us know about the delay? The answers quickly reveal a liar.

We suspected that the employee was lying to cover his tardiness so we thought of a series of questions that would be difficult to answer without actually experiencing an automotive breakdown. This is what cross-examination is all about. The answers demonstrate untruthfulness.

There are countless examples of law enforcement officers being caught on cross-examination being untruthful, just as there are countless examples of defendants being caught being untruthful. Most witnesses will nuance their testimony, meaning that they know the goal of their testimony, and so they shade their testimony toward that end. For example, a driver is arrested for reckless driving. The passenger in the vehicle is a friend of the defendant. If the passenger were to testify about the manner in which the vehicle was being driven he or she would probably testify that the vehicle was traveling at a safe and reasonable speed. The arresting officer might testify that the vehicle was traveling at a high rate of speed and was exceeding the speed limit. Sounds as if someone is lying, but in reality, both witnesses are probably correct if the vehicle was traveling at 57 mph in a posted 55 mph zone, with a road traffic safety study indicated that most vehicles travel at 58.2 mph on that road. Both witnesses are telling their version of the truth, but they nuance their testimony to help their respective sides.

A judge can intervene during cross-examination to protect an officer. Judges can declare a recess right in the middle of that Perry Mason moment so that the Officer will have a chance to consult with the prosecutor during the break to develop some plausible response to that final question which is inevitably coming based upon the line of questioning just interrupted by the judge.

There is United States Supreme Court legal authority for the proposition that a judge can order a witness not to speak to anyone, including his attorney, during a fortuitous break in cross-examination. Interestingly, the United States Supreme Court case I mention involves the defendant in a murder case being ordered not to talk to anyone during a break. The United States Supreme Court opinion explains how this ruling avoids coaching of the defendant and encourages more truthful testimony. For some reason, most judges are unwilling to use this legal authority when it comes to ordering a police officer not to speak to anyone during a break in their cross-examination.

The reason for the break or delay in a trial can also be used by the judge to influence the jury. Trial departments are usually busy places. During a trial, there might be jurors deliberating in the jury room from the trial just completed on the previous day. The trial judge might also have other duties and assignments in addition to trials. Most judges use discretion and will simply tell a jury that the trial will be starting thirty minutes late the next morning because the judge has "other matters" to handle in the morning. However, some judges will tell a jury, who must decide guilty or innocence, that the trial will commence thirty minutes late in the morning because the judge has three "sentencing matters." This information is really unnecessary and seems to needlessly focus the jury on the frequency of guilty verdicts and seems to normalize sentencing hearings, making a verdict of guilty seem that much easier and common.

Judicial Time Management

When a defendant chooses to testify, the prosecutor often is taken by surprise because you can never be certain what the defense will be. Sometimes the defendant's testimony will be obvious based upon the charges. In a battery case if the defendant testifies, he will almost always testify that the victim was the aggressor, and the prosecutor starts the trial knowing this and is prepared. Prior to the trial the prosecutor will often gather the height and weight of the victim and defendant in order to argue who is more likely to have been the aggressor. Small people are less likely to pick fights with big people is a very flawed argument, but if the victim is larger the prosecutor will never mention the information and so the defense attorney will often bring it up.

But what if the case is an armed robbery case with three eyewitnesses who identified the defendant and the defendant takes the witness stand and starts telling the jury about his evil twin brother who just moved to town from another state who recently had a large amount of cash. Before the defendant can finish his last sentence the defense attorney tells the defendant thank you and sits down. The judge turns to the prosecutor with a grin, because he knows the story is outrageous, and says, "cross?"

Cross-examination can be a difficult art form. Experience and the ability to think on your feet are critical to a successful cross-examination. How in the world would you digest this story and start firing out questions in the time it takes to walk from the counsel table to the podium? What do you ask? How old is your brother? What is his name? Date of birth? Where does he live? Under the pressure of the courtroom, with a jury staring at you, it can be a struggle.

If a judge sees that the prosecution is struggling with the defense story *de jur* the judge might just declare, "I see it's getting late, let's take our recess for the day and reconvene tomorrow." This allows the prosecutor plenty of time to think about his approach and to have the police run a check on any relatives of the defendant. The interruption is at four o'clock and the usual courtroom schedule is five o'clock, but the judge wants to help the prosecution prepare a more effective cross-examination.

The judge can slow the pace of cross-examination to assist the officer. Direct examination involves obvious questions and answers that have usually been rehearsed with the witness outside the presence of the jury. Cross-examination usually involves a faster pace of questioning so that the witness answers truthfully and has less time to think about what the answer should be, to better suit his narrative. If the prosecution witness begins to blurt out stupid answers without thinking about the ramifications of those answers, the judge can instantly step in with a claim that the court reporter is having trouble keeping up and will ask the defense attorney to slow down. The judicial intervention is really twofold. The judge is telling the defense attorney to slow down with a bogus claim that the court reporter is having difficulty, but the judge is also trying to inappropriately help the officer by hinting that the officer can also slow down and think before answering.

The judicial interruptions to the pace will become progressively more authoritative and distracting. Counsel! I have asked you to slow down. The court reporter is having trouble keeping up with you, the judge will again claim. This is usually the only point in the trial where the judge expresses concern for the court reporter. If the matter is recorded via audio then the judge will not attempt this ploy - usually.

When the judge tries to use the court report as a pretext for slowing the cross-examination of the officer, the reporter is under pressure to agree. Many times the court reporter, who is usually not assigned to that courtroom, will indicate that everything is fine and the pace of the questions is manageable. They proudly want everyone in the courtroom to know that they have polished skills and can keep up. But most of the time, usually when the court reporter is permanently assigned to the courtroom, the reporter will follow the lead of the judge and will confirm that he or she is having difficulty keeping up. If the court reporter is assigned to the judge then they usually agree that the pace is too fast. If the reporter is a floater and is assigned wherever needed, then the pace is usually not too fast. Being agreeable with a suggestion from your "boss" is nothing new. Technically, the court reporter works for the court and not the judge, but there is little doubt about who is in charge.

How slow do you have to talk to make the judge feel like he was successful in helping out the prosecution witness? Well a long, long, time ago in my youthful exuberance I defiantly and sarcastically modified my speech so severely that it was as if I was speaking like Tarzan in the jungle - me Tarzan, you Jane. As you can imagine, it is difficult to be effective under these circumstances. The judge was pissed off and called a sidebar. But the judge used the court reporter for everything and so the court reporter was at sidebar. I tried to complain to the judge about the alleged difficulty the court reporter was having as he tried his best to scold me for my courtroom demeanor.

I tried to negotiate and asked that we not use the court reporter and I offered to tape record the proceedings so that we have a record of events in the unlikely event of an appeal. Request Denied!

So sometimes it's the court reporter trying to sabotage the defense attorney with the consent and acquiescence of the judge, and sometimes it's the judge trying to sabotage the defense attorney using the court report as his ploy.

The judge can also intervene by simply interrupting your question with his own discretionary objection and telling you to move on to your next question. For example, imagine the officer testifies on direct examination that the suspect's vehicle was yellow. Upon cross-examination you ask the officer about the color of the suspect's car and now he claims the car was red. You ask the officer in the most embarrassing, loud, Perry Mason, gotcha, voice, "Didn't you just testify twenty minutes ago on direct examination, under oath, that the car was YELLOW! The judge burst out in a loud thunderous voice, "Counsel! The officer has already testified as to the color of the car. Now MOVE ON to your next question! The judge has saved the day for the prosecutor and has stolen your Perry Mason moment leaving you to point out the discrepancy in your closing argument.

Relevant Witnesses

The evidence code is complicated and confusing. The evidence code includes rules which govern trials and define permissible and impermissible evidence at trial. The responsibility for interpreting those rules, and judicial discretion, provide an opportunity for judges to manipulate the outcome of a jury trial. In particular, the rule of evidence regarding the relevancy of evidence provides an interesting opportunity for judicial abuse.

There is a seemingly innocuous rule of evidence that states that only relevant evidence is admissible. This rule would apply to both written and testimonial evidence, therefore, no witness may testify unless that testimony is relevant. First, you might be thinking about why in the world there would be such an obvious rule. I don't know and I'm too lazy to research the legislative history of the rule. Second, and more importantly, you might be thinking about how in the world a judge could possibly think of a way to use such a common sense rule against the defense attorney?

Imagine a jury trial where the defendant is on trial for murder. The defendant murdered his bowling league rival at the bowling alley. The prosecutor presents an eyewitness to the killing, a detective, and a crime lab employee. The names, titles, and business addresses of all of these witnesses were disclosed to the defense attorney long before the trial started in accordance with the trial rules. In addition, all of these witnesses were disclosed to the judge at the start of the trial so that the judge could ask the potential jurors if any of the witnesses were known to them.

After the prosecutor concludes presenting evidence from the three witnesses, the defense attorney has an opportunity to present evidence. The defense attorney calls famous golfer Tiger Woods to the stand. The legal birth name of Tiger Woods is "Eldrick Tont Woods" and this name was disclosed to the prosecutor and judge prior to the trial. Tiger takes the stand and the defense attorney starts asking questions about the defendant's golfing abilities. This is followed by more golf questions, and yet more questions about the defendant's most recent golf scores. The prosecutor, judge, and jurors start displaying a puzzled, curious facial expression.

The prosecutor stands and declares, "objection, relevancy." The judge responds by saying, "sustained." The judge asks both attorneys to come to sidebar. The judge asks the defense attorney, out of the earshot of the jury, if the defendant discussed the murders with Mr. Woods on the golf course. The defense attorney looks surprised by the questions and tells the judge it was never discussed. The judge asks the defense attorney if it was his contention that this murder occurred on the golf course, and not the bowling alley as the prosecution witness testified. The defense attorney quickly responded that it was not his contention. The judge, looking exasperated at this point, asks the defense attorney why this witness was in court testifying. The defense attorney responds that Tiger is a great golfer and he thought his testimony was interesting, entertaining, and jurors would be less likely to believe a murder was committed by a golfer such as the defendant.

The judge promptly excuses the witness ruling that the testimony is not relevant to the issues presented by the case. Obviously, this type of situation almost never happens and the parties always call relevant witnesses to provide testimony in support of their positions, although on rare occasions a mentally ill self-represented defendant does try to embark on this type of bizarre witness journey. I am always amused when the *pro per* defendants send witness subpoenas to all of the judges at the courthouse, or try to call the President of the United States as a witness.

So, how can the prosecutor and the judge take advantage of such an evidentiary rule to gain an advantage in a trial? There are no depositions in criminal cases. In civil cases witnesses are identified and disclosed. The parties then take the deposition of those witnesses to learn what the witness knows about the case. The deposition is recorded so that it can be compared and contrasted with subsequent trial testimony if necessary. In criminal cases, the police officer writes a report which is disclosed to the defense attorney prior to trial. The defense attorney knows that the officer will memorize the report and will generally testify consistently with the report. If there are civilian witnesses then the officers will obtain their statements and will include those in the report.

Sometimes it is discovered during the testimony of a witness at trial that an officer intentionally failed to include exculpatory information in the witness statement. For example, an officer interviews a witness who describes seeing an object in the defendant's hand. The officer asks the witness if the object was a gun, but the witness is unsure. Later in the interview, after the officer tells the witness that the defendant was found with a gun, the witness agrees with the officer that the object seen in his hand could have been a gun. When the officer writes the report it includes a statement that the witness observed a gun in the hand of the defendant. However, when the witness testifies at trial the truth is revealed and the witness again asserts uncertainty about the object being a gun.

If the defense attorney calls a witness to testify at trial then their testimony is generally unknown to the prosecutor because there are usually no written witness statements. When defense attorneys initially interview a potential witness they are normally very cautious about what they write down because all notes of the conversation must be turned over to the prosecutor once the witness is disclosed to the prosecutor. Therefore, defense attorneys frequently do not take notes when they speak to witnesses to avoid turning those notes over to the prosecutor.

So, once a defense witness is disclosed to the prosecutor, the prosecutor will often immediately have a law enforcement investigator contact the disclosed witness to try to interview them in order to find out the details of their testimony. Knowing what a defense witness will say on the stand in front of the jury prior to trial is an advantage. This information allows the prosecutor to prepare his cross-examination of the witness, assists in preparing rebuttal evidence, and provides insight into the defense strategy.

Some unscrupulous defense attorneys will fail to disclose witnesses until the day of trial, or even after the trial has commenced. When asked about the failure to disclose the witness by the judge, the defense attorney disingenuously claims that the decision to call the witness was a last minute tactical trial decision. The judge will not be able to prove that the defense attorney knew he was going to use the witness long before trial, but if the witness turns out to be a critical witness for the defense, then the necessity of the witness becomes obvious and the prosecutor and judge know the defense attorney is playing games.

Once a defense witness is disclosed, the chess game continues, because the defense attorney knows that the prosecutor might attempt to contact the defense witness. Therefore, the defense attorney, prior to disclosing the witness, will often advise the witness about the disclosure. The defense attorney is not permitted to tell a witness not to talk to the prosecutor or the investigator. However, the defense attorney may advise the witness that they have no obligation to provide a statement, and that they have every right not to speak to the prosecutor if they choose not to do so.

In summary, defense witnesses are disclosed to the prosecutor prior to trial. However, there is almost never a written statement from a defense witnesses, and they almost never agree to speak to the prosecutor or investigator about their testimony, or anything else.

So how can the prosecutor take the deposition of the defense witness or find out what the witness will say during the trial? The old evidence code "relevancy" trick provides the mechanism for disclosure. Prior to the defense witness testifying, the prosecutor will tell the judge that the defense attorney has provided a witness list and that there is a name which is unknown and not mentioned in the police report. The prosecutor will disingenuously tell the judge that he has no idea what this witness will testify to and that his testimony may not be relevant. The prosecutor will argue that a hearing should be held in order to determine the relevancy of the testimony.

Again, the judge has a great deal of discretion in handling the prosecution request. Most judges will appear annoyed by the ridiculous charade and will generically ask the defense attorney, "who is Mr. Defense Witness?" The defense attorney will respond that Mr. Defense Witness is a neighbor who observed the shooting in this case. The judge might then give a cold stare at the prosecutor and might say something like, "there ya have it. His testimony is relevant."

However, some judges, who want to help the prosecutor, will actively participate in the charade and will ask the defense attorney about the testimony.

Judge: What is Mr. Defense Witness going to say during his testimony?
Defense: He saw the shooting and so he is a relevant witness, your honor.

Judge: And who did he see shoot?
Defense: He saw the defendant do the shooting, your honor.

Judge: And what else will he testify to?
Defense: Well, I can't be sure exactly what he will say, you honor. (The defense attorney wants to provide as little information as possible which will assist the prosecutor.)

Judge: Well if he says anything else then I might exclude it since it was not disclosed to me, or I might determine it is not relevant, and as an officer of the court I am ordering you to disclose what you expect the witness will say on the stand.
Defense: Well, your honor, he might say that he saw the victim holding a gun to the defendant's head. Then he saw a struggle. Then he saw the defendant wrestle the gun away

92

from the victim. Then he saw the victim attack the defendant. Then he saw the defendant shoot the victim and he heard a loud bang.

Judge: I see. Okay Mr. Prosecutor, I think you have everything you need. I will allow the evidence which appears relevant to the case.

Now the prosecutor calls the investigating detective to discuss the anticipated testimony, and tries to figure out some plan to undermine the witness' credibility. The prosecutor will also run a criminal history check on the witness to see if he has any criminal convictions, or is on probation or parole. All of which can be used by the prosecutor and his investigator to pressure, intimidate, and dissuade the potential witness. The judge has used the evidence code as a charade to force the defense attorney into disclosing the self-defense theory which is obviously a monumental advantage for the prosecutor.

Some judges will actually hold the hearing so the prosecutor can learn even more about the witness and the anticipated testimony. This also gives the prosecutor a better chance of using the courthouse atmosphere to intimidate the witness into speaking to the investigator in the hallway before or after the hearing.

Chapter 7: Reading the Jury Instructions

Jury instructions are the set of rules that a jury is expected to follow when deciding a case. Jury instructions are given to the jury by the judge who will read them aloud in open court. There can be disputes about which instructions to give, and which portions apply, but instructions on the law from the judge are so important to the determination of the jury that an error provides a real opportunity for a successful appeal. Therefore, judges are very cautious about how they try to bias the jury via jury instructions.

The instructions are read aloud exactly as written to avoid any particular emphasis on one instruction over another, and to avoid any possible prejudicial comments or goofy explanations by local judges. However, after reading and hearing the instructions hundreds of times by hundreds of judges you start to observe that some judges still manage to find a way to read the exact text, and place vocal emphasis on a particular portion, or modify the meaning slightly by the way they read the text.

For example, imagine an instruction with a series of conditions. In order for you to reach a verdict of guilty, the prosecutor has the burden to convince you of A, B, C, and D. The distinct conditions are all separated with a comma and any reader fluent in English would normally pause momentarily between the clauses due to the commas. However, many judges with years of experience will intentionally read this instruction in a monotone machine gun fashion which intentionally de-emphasizes the separate nature of the conditions. There is no appellate remedy as long the judge reads the exact text.

Incidentally, the jury does receive an exact copy of the instructions which are sent into the jury deliberation room with the jurors.

What if the judge rolls his eyes and shakes his head as he reads some of the jury instructions? The judge will submit a declaration denying that he did anything improper and the bailiff might be asked to submit a corroborating declaration claiming that he watched the judge throughout the reading of the entire jury instructions and the judge did nothing improper. Appeal denied.

Chapter 8: Closing Argument

By the time closing argument arrives the damage is usually done. The jury has already been steered by the judge toward a verdict. However, if you make a great closing argument then the judge can again intervene to change the tide.

Prosecutor Goes First

Attention spans are short and seem to be getting shorter in a high-tech, media filled world. There are reasons why high school and college classes usually last less than an hour. The prosecutor is allowed to make the first closing argument at the end of the trial which means an advantage to the prosecutor because the jurors start fading out after the conclusion of the prosecution filibuster of guilt.

After the prosecutor concludes his closing argument the judge would then turn to me and invite me to make my closing argument. It would take me a few minutes to set up easels and diagrams and so I would tell the judge I needed a few minutes and would ask him to allow the jury to stand and stretch if they choose. I always had the impression that the judge had not heard the request before from other defense attorneys but they would always agree since it would be difficult for the judge to deny such a request in front of the jurors. The seventh inning stretch works in baseball and I always felt it allowed me to really change the tone set by the prosecutor and to freshen up the jurors.

Equal Time Limits

Often the judge will set time limits on the closing argument. Time limits sound perfectly fair and impartial because each side is given equal time. However, because the prosecution and defense have to prove or establish different things, the time it takes to accomplish those things is very different and so time limits almost always hurt the defense and help the prosecutor.

In closing argument the prosecutor might need only a few minutes to reference the relevant law as given in the jury instructions, and to recite the facts which establish the law has been violated. On the other hand, the defense might need to challenge a prosecution witness as not credible by comparing and contrasting his various statements in the course of the trial with his statements to the arresting agency. This type of analysis can be laborious and time consuming which can further limit time spent during closing argument in other beneficial areas.

Just the Facts

During closing argument the prosecutor and the defense attorney will reference the law and the facts of the case. Each side is permitted to argue about the facts, and is permitted to argue about reasonable inferences from those facts. However, it is not permissible to invent facts during closing argument.

At the end of a trial the parties are never completely satisfied, and always wish the facts were more compelling toward establishing either guilt or innocence. Occasionally, a party will intentionally, or mistakenly, recite inaccurate facts during their closing argument in order to be more persuasive to the jury. The other party normally would then object to the misstatement of the evidence which then compels the judge to make some sort of ruling, or instruct the jury accordingly. This provides an ideal final opportunity to shape the outcome of the jury.

Let me provide an example of how a factual dispute in closing argument can be manipulated by the judge. During the closing argument the prosecutor tells the jury that the defendant owns a blue car, and that the store owner testified that the robber left the scene in a blue car. Actually, the store owner testified that the car was a dark color, and the prosecutor asked the store owner if it could have been blue, and the store owner responded that the car "might have been blue."

The defense attorney objects to the prosecutor's argument and interrupts by saying, OBJECTION! Your honor, the prosecutor is misstating the facts. The witness testified that the vehicle was a dark color, and said it might have been blue only after the prosecutors' suggestion.

The judge has a lot of discretion in terms of how he responds to this legal objection. As you have seen throughout this book, judicial discretion creates opportunities for judges to influence the outcome of a trial.

A very typical, common, generic, impartial response would be the following: Ladies and gentlemen of the jury, you have heard all the evidence. It is up to you to determine the facts of the case. You may rely on your notes and your own memory to assist you in determining the facts. You are the fact finders and sole judge of whether a party is misstating the evidence. Proceed counsel.

This is a paraphrase of a speech I have heard countless times over the years. If I wandered into a trial during closing argument and I heard the judge recite something similar to this speech, I would instantly conclude that the judge was probably a fair and honest judge.

Let me describe another possible response to the objection. The prosecutor makes the statement about the blue car, the defense attorney makes the same objection, the judge looks visibly annoyed and responds as follows: Counsel! Please do not interrupt with speaking objections! I would ask both attorneys to try not to interrupt one another during closing argument. Counsel, my recollection is that the car was blue as well. Objection overruled!

The judge's response accomplished several things to help the prosecutor. First, the defense attorney would now feel very intimidated to object again, and so the prosecutor now knows that it is possible to twist the facts even further. Second, the judge has diminished the credibility of the defense attorney by telling the jury that the prosecutor is right and the defense attorney is wrong. Third, the judge has communicated to the jury that the defense attorney has done something improper by objecting which diminishes his credibility and trust in the minds of the jurors. Lastly, most jurors will now believe the car was blue, despite the testimony of the witness.

Chapter 9: A New Trial Sounds Appealing

Mulligans are not allowed after a criminal jury trial. In golf, if you hit your golf ball into the woods, your buddies will often let you try the shot again without incurring a penalty - a Mulligan. After a criminal jury trial, you do not get a new trial simply because you do not like the outcome.

Many people mistakenly believe that you can appeal a criminal jury trial verdict if you disagree with the outcome. However, in order to win an appeal, and receive a new trial from the appellate court, you must generally establish that something improper happened during the course of the trial which significantly affected the outcome. There are many types of appellate issues, but if you think the trial judge made prejudicial errors during the course of the trial, then you would commonly file an appeal with the Appellate Court seeking a new trial.

Appellate law is a very complicated and specialized area of law which requires a great deal of experience and expertise. Representing a client in a criminal appeal requires knowledge of many special procedures, laws, deadlines, and rules. Most criminal defense attorneys who represent clients in jury trials are usually not sufficiently competent to handle an appeal, and so the client is referred to an attorney who specializes in appeals. Appellate attorneys are very boring, they love to write, they all wear glasses, they have no sense of humor, and they all hate puppies. However, appellate attorneys do not believe in stereotypes.

Should you file an appeal if the judge does something wrong at trial? It depends upon what the judge did and what you want to achieve.

100

For example, if the judge made insulting comments to the defense attorney or the client, outside the presence of the jury, then it would not be appropriate to seek relief from the Court of Appeals regarding the verdict because the verdict would not have been impacted by the comments. In this situation, a letter to the presiding judge explaining the situation will often curb future abuses by the judge. However, if the judge imposed an unduly harsh sentence after the verdict, then it would be appropriate to file an appeal regarding the sentencing issue. The appeal would not seek a new trial, but instead, would seek a new sentencing, and the issue would be whether the judge's insults established a bias and prejudice toward the defendant that would make it unfair for the judge to determine a fair sentence.

Sometimes there is no appellate remedy for insults by a judge at sentencing. The media will frequently follow high profile murder cases and most people have seen the coverage on the local television news programs. Often you will see coverage of a judge during a sentencing hearing. The judge will scowl at the defendant and will chastise and reprimand the defendant telling him he is a cold blooded killer who took the life of an innocent person who was loved by his family and friends who are all present in the courtroom for the sentencing. This is followed by the judge imposing a life sentence in prison. So how does the judge get away with this? Isn't the judge proving on the record that he or she cannot be fair and impartial for the sentencing? Nope, in these types of sentencing hearings the entire hearing is a charade for the benefit of the friends and family of the victim. The judge is putting on a show for everyone in the community and is playing to the cameras for reelection time. If a judge uses this type of language on the bench it is only because the judge has no sentencing discretion. The only sentence the judge can legally impose is imprisonment for life. Therefore, it doesn't matter what the judge says in court because the defendant cannot appeal the sentence of life imprisonment arguing an abuse of discretion theory, because the judge did not exercise any discretion imposing the sentence.

When the judge has sentencing discretion you will often see the defendant make a plea of leniency to the judge, and you will see the judge tone down their comments to avoid an appeal for being biased against the defendant.

An appeal is generally reserved for situations where the judge makes a mistake regarding the law. For example, if the judge instructed the jury in a criminal case that they may convict the defendant if they believe the evidence of his guilt was established by a preponderance of the evidence, instead of beyond a reasonable doubt. In this instance, the judges' error on the standard of guilt would be so critical to the determination of the jury that a new trial must be granted.

In less common situations, it is possible that the judge acts so prejudicial toward the defendant that it demonstrates a clear bias and is so prejudicial that the verdict might reasonably have been impacted by the misconduct of the judge. For example, if the judge refers to the defendant as the "guilty guy" throughout the trial then this type of behavior would warrant a new trial. Although, I can think of some appellate judges trying to deny the defendant a new trial by arguing that the judge read the jury instruction to the jurors at the end of the trial that instructed them that they alone were responsible for determining guilty or innocence. Yes, the "guilty guy" comment by the judge results in a new trial.

But most judges know the standards and boundaries and the standard upon which many judicial officers self-regulate their behavior is the appellate standard. What can I say or do, on and off the record, to get this jury where I want them to be, without getting overturned on appeal? There is no appellate remedy when judges use their discretion to influence the outcome of a jury trial as described throughout this book. Many of the examples and situations described in this book are so subtle, undetectable, and difficult to prove, that an appellate court would not be convinced that a new trial was legally warranted.

Each state has a mechanism for supervising judges. In California, judicial conduct is regulated via The Commission on Judicial Performance. This state agency is responsible for investigating complaints of judicial misconduct and judicial incapacity and for disciplining judges. The commission's mandate is to protect the public, enforce standards of judicial conduct and maintain public confidence in the integrity and independence of the judicial system.

The commission's jurisdiction includes all judges of California's Superior Courts and the justices of the Court of Appeal and Supreme Court. The commission also has jurisdiction over former judges for conduct prior to retirement or resignation. Additionally, the commission shares authority with the Superior Courts for the oversight of court commissioners and referees. The commission does not have authority over Federal Judges, judges pro tem or private judges.

The commission's authority is limited to investigating allegations of judicial misconduct and, if warranted, imposing discipline. Judicial misconduct usually involves conduct in conflict with the standards set forth in the Code of Judicial Ethics.

The commission cannot change a decision made by any judicial officer; this is a function of the state's appellate courts. After investigation and in some cases a public hearing, the commission may impose sanctions ranging from confidential discipline to removal from office.

Chapter 10: The Requiem

Judges are supposed to be fair and impartial. They are not supposed to take sides, and they do not determine the verdict in a criminal trial - the jury decides.

When a judge sets his mind toward steering and influencing a jury, the verdict is usually a forgone conclusion. Words, gestures, facial expressions, legal rulings, court procedures, and so much more, all combine to create a powerful suggestion intentionally created to move the minds of the jurors. If you believe in fair and impartial juries deciding cases, then it is important to become enlightened about the ways in which juries can be easily manipulated by those entrusted to safeguard the process.

For those of you who might be apathetic about judicial intervention, I would ask you to consider the ramifications of such intervention. The erosion of the protection afforded to citizens by a jury trial is of little concern to some, until they, or someone close to them, is charged with a crime. If you place your trust in the jury trial system and feel that the jury reaches the correct result 99% of the time, then you also must accept that the jury trial system wrongly convicts hundreds, or even thousands of people each year. Wrongful convictions are statistically rare, but I have never met an experienced criminal defense attorney who is not aware of several innocent clients being wrongly convicted by a jury.

Jury trials are inherently flawed and are vulnerable to many types of manipulations by the trial judge, but I can't think of a better system than trial by jury. With more than two decades of trial experience, I can envision many reforms which would improve the jury trial process, but no improvement would be as significant as making changes toward ensuring fair and impartial judges. Obviously, the political process plays a critical role in ensuring fair jury trials. The appointment of judges who preside over criminal trials is a very important and serious matter. Voters need to carefully consider who they vote for in local judicial elections, because judges have discretion which allows them to impact the outcome of trials. Ultimately, the voting public must decide who best serves the community at the courthouse.

There are many honest, fair and impartial judges on the bench presiding over jury trials. There are many former prosecutors who have abandoned their former allegiance and have embraced their neutral role in the jury trial process. But there are many on the bench who choose to tamper with the process because they genuinely believe they know the correct outcome for the case and in their eyes it is important that the jury "gets it right," meaning that the verdict is consistent with their view of the case.

But this mindset misses the point of the Sixth Amendment of the United States Constitution. We do not want verdicts decided by one King, or one President, or one local judge.

It is finished.

www.ingramcontent.com/pod-product-compliance
Lightning Source LLC
Chambersburg PA
CBHW032008190326
41520CB00007B/404